STRUGGLING WELL
THANKS FOR ASKING

SHARING OUR STORIES TO HELP YOU FIND COMFORT AND ENHANCE YOUR JOURNEY

EXPRESS YOURSELF PUBLISHING

CONTENTS

INTRODUCTION

**A slice of real life
As Told by real champions
Positive women**

Before we begin, I would like to explain the title of the book. It is a little tongue in cheek, but it is meant to address a very, very, very complicated issue—WIDOWHOOD. I know when you hear the word widow, you think, so, her husband died, what's the big deal? Well, I'll explain the BIG DEAL.

If you look up the word struggle, it says, "adj. fighting or having difficulty working through obstacles to achieve a goal." Let me explain the word obstacles. If you google Life's Problems, you will see this list.

Emptiness

Friendship

Health

Unfair Treatment

Inner Peace

Failure

Financial Crisis

Mental Health

Any one of these struggles on their own is hard work to overcome, but when you become a widow, all of these problems kick in all at once! So you can see what we are talking about. We added the word WELL in our title because with love and a knowledgeable community helping, the job is more manageable! Feel our love and support, and through our shared experiences, take away comfort knowing you are not alone. Be safe. Nurture yourself. Pat yourself on the back. Only deal with those who "get it". Give yourself hugs. Learn to meditate. Give thanks when things are going well, get enough sleep and exercise and nourishment, work on your talents, and don't forget to wear your makeup!

IN ORDER TO GET THE MOST OUT OF THIS BOOK I'D LIKE TO MAKE A FEW SUGGESTIONS

1. You do not have to read all the stories at once.

2. Find a quiet space at a time where there will be no interruptions--maybe the same time each day.

3. Have a paper and pencil to write any thoughts that may be helpful.

4. Open the Table of Contents and pick a title that appeals to you.

Enjoy

Since each story is different it is best to digest one at a time as they may apply to you.

THANKS FOR ASKING!

NOW WE CAN BEGIN

A post-traumatic brain is a challenge. It forgets time. It forgets details. It can make you sit and stare at nothing for long periods. Where did I put that? Did I send out that bill? What day is it? Do I have to think of what to make for dinner? Why do I need to buy food? It blocks out extraneous noise, and it can't focus long enough to read. It goes blank without warning, and it replays upsetting thoughts. Someday it hopes to join the so-called real world. It's a work in progress.

I attended a few groups, but I didn't last. I just couldn't listen to the sad stories all the time. The same people would go over the same sadness weekly with no goals in sight. I felt worse sometimes when I left. But things changed when I went to a funeral. I was still in my stage if you looked at me, I said, "My husband died." Luckily the person I said it to was an employee at the funeral home, and she mentioned that they could sponsor a bereavement facilitator at my synagogue. This stroke of luck turned into two six-week sessions with a core group of women that developed a real bond and good energy.

When the sessions ended, I asked the membership person if we could continue to meet on our own, and she said, "you can continue if you lead the group." Me lead the group? Wow! I guess I could. But I was still healing myself. I mobilized my teaching experience, and it's now over ten years that we have had a fabulous group of women who have developed strength and friendships. We've done wonderful creative things together. And now we've published a book! WHO WOULD HAVE DREAMED?????

We've had amazing articles written about us in the Inquirer, The Exponent, and Corporation for Aging. We were on TV on the Suzanne Roberts Show and Channel 6, The Art of Aging. We've had chair yoga teachers, art teachers, English teas, and social excursions as we gained strength and new perspectives about ourselves.

We explored the art of haikus, the art of 5, 7, 5. So much emotion can come out of 17 syllables. The poems have become a creative and healing tool for us. Feelings are targeted and expressed powerfully. Throughout the book, you will see a number of these poems written by our insightful and brave women

Hopefully, our words will set the stage for the inspiration necessary to guide you.

Enjoy this quote. "Sometimes when you think you are buried, you are just being planted!!!" You gotta believe!!!"

As we focus on healing, we will celebrate who we are and the realization of who we have become. We will get to our destination safely—so FASTEN YOUR SEATBELTS AS WE TAKE OFF ON THE ROAD TO RECOVERY

From the bottom of my heart, I want to thank all of the women who have contributed their stories. I am so proud of all of you. We came together by chance at a very difficult time in all of our lives. We found safety and strength at our regular widow support meetings and have worked very hard to become our best selves.

I LOVE YOU LADIES

In addition: We would like to thank Rabbi Eli Freedman of Rodeph Shalom Synagogue and Rabbi Robert Leib of Old York Road Temple-Beth Am, for their love and support. We are grateful for your belief in our mission to help people heal.

Will I survive this
The pain is unbearable
I feel paralyzed

What hat do you wear
Victim or superhero
It will be your choice

Life moves in cycles
Hardships and pleasures alike
But we must ride them

Once upon a time
Happily ever after
Is that how it goes

I will survive this
I will use the love I have
To build a strong life

I am confident
I am becoming brand new
Full of positive

A CONVERSATION

JUST IN CASE YOU DON'T KNOW

CEECEE

He was my North, my South, my East and West,

My working week and my Sunday rest,

My noon, my midnight, my talk, my song; (H.
W. Auden, "Funeral Blues")

You were my everything. We were married for almost fifty years. We grew up together. We were children when we formed our union. It has been so hard to give up, my person.

After a lifetime
For one half decade alone
How I miss together

Certain things surrounding your dying still remain vivid. Having to give you morphine to ease the pain terrified me. I am not trained as a nurse. Taking you to doctors, asking questions; that I could do. But this other thing took every ounce of my courage. I also remember that night, two days before you died, when you jumped out of bed and ran into the living room. I ran following you, and heard you say, "We have to hurry, I am going on a trip." Many experts believe that those who are dying often mention taking a trip. After that episode, I knew that your end was near.

After your death, I was occupied for long months with all that needed to be accomplished.

That business was a blessing. It gave me direction and kept my mind on task. I think I was on remote for close to two years.

So how am I doing now, you ask? (Though I like to think, you may already know.)

I definitely feel lonely, but I also feel great joy. I have tackled challenges, reached out to others, kept some important long-term relationships, and made several new friends.

Let me tell you about two of my newest friends. They are our grandchildren. Hannah is just two and one-half. She is full of life and very curious. Some mornings after she is dressed, she tells her parents, "Goodbye, I am going to work." When asked where she works, she says,

"The museum." Hannah has her career goals set since she loves children's museums.

Jillian is almost eight months old, and she is the smiliest baby around. I am getting to know this calm and sweet natured person who adores her big sister. You would love them both, and be so proud.

I remember how sad you were because you wouldn't know your grandchildren. You expected that they would come one day, but not until after you were gone.

I shed tears for you
What a Pop-Pop you would be
You missed those births

I want you to know that you will be a part of our grandchildren's lives by the pictures we show them, and the stories we tell.

As you can see, I am very excited about these little girls, but what else is new, you ask?

I have big plans for the future when the Pandemic really eases up. (That is another story for some other time.) I hope to restart in-person classes, attend live theater, and travel again.

Though I have never been a big fan of experiencing things alone, I will push myself to do more on my own. I might even try out a new hobby that involves using my body. The theme of my life now is to continue being open to new experiences.

> I am on the verge
> Of becoming someone new
> I am not sure who

So, though I keep struggling, I do look forward to the future. I will, however, check in with you from time to time. In the last line of the verse from Auden's poem, he says

"I thought that love would last forever: I was wrong."

Ah, but love does last forever, not in the physical sense, but in our hearts.

You will always be a part of me. In that sense, I know that you are present in my life.

When I am tackling something challenging, I ask for your help and I believe that you are encouraging me. Because of that, I am certain that you are still sending me your love.

P.S. How do you like my haikus? They are a new endeavor.

AND JUST LIKE THAT...

CINDY H.

WHEN BAD THINGS HAPPEN TO GOOD PEOPLE

The journey of widowhood began for me at age 61.

The bell rang at my shore house early on Sunday morning of memorial weekend. At the door was a police officer. My fleeting thought in that moment was—they're here to tell me I can't park my car on the street, blocking my own driveway. But that was not the case. Jay was in a bike accident, struck by a car, and was being rushed to the hospital. He was unresponsive at the scene. My worst nightmare had actually come to be.

Jay was an avid biker. He loved being out on the open road down the shore, taking in the air and the scenery while enjoying the exercise. He was also a very conscientious, safe biker who took all precautions and took classes to learn how to change a spare and repair bike parts so he'd always be prepared out on the road. He couldn't have prepared for this.

My life and that of my kids, my family, was forever changed that day. Jay suffered a severe, global brain injury. We sat vigil in the ICU for days, in an alternate universe, in a time warp, while Jay remained in a coma, on a ventilator and feeding tube. He never woke up. Of one thing doctors were certain: he would not improve. Of another, they had no idea: how long Jay might remain alive. Then, just like that, after 22 days, he died. His life ended.

I share this brief background about my loss because it was a shocking, overwhelming trauma to everyone who loved Jay. In an instant, my life came to a screeching halt. After the funeral and Shiva that followed, I recall thinking, *I don't know how to live my life now.* It felt as if someone had simply come along and wiped out my future, taking an eraser to the blackboard and throwing away the chalk. My future felt blank, bleak, empty. Life had dealt Jay, and therefore me, the most unjust blow. We were robbed of growing old together, robbed of our future plans, and robbed of shared joyous occasions we wished for our kids.

But somehow, inexplicably, life goes on, and so did we. Despite the bewilderment, trying to make sense of a tragic, unimaginable loss, I plugged ahead and just kept putting one foot in front of the other. After spending the summer in a fog, I gratefully returned to my teaching job in the fall.

ME, MYSELF AND I

Shortly after Jay's passing, my sister shared her words of encouragement with me to assure me I was going to be okay. In part, I believe she was trying to assure *herself* that I was going to be okay. She outlined the four reasons: I have terrific kids, a wide circle of supportive friends, a good job, and financial security. She was right about all of that, and I could recognize how fortunate I was to be in those circumstances. Even in the midst of despair, I could acknowledge I was 'lucky'.

Nonetheless, no one could imagine what it took to wake up each morning, simply get out of bed and face the day ahead. How much energy it required to put on my 'war paint' and go to work; how much strength and patience it took to manage new, uncharted territory alone. Yes, alone. Because no matter how strong or large my support group of friends and family was, at the end of the day, every day, alone is where I found myself. Sometimes I felt like I was sinking into an abyss, with no clue how to dig myself out of it.

In a way, work was my salvation, offering me structure and an anchor around which to build a new life. It was a safe place, so to speak, where I had always operated independently of Jay. Yet when I'd get into my car at day's end, I felt nearly paralyzed. I'd sit quietly for a while before even starting the engine, just trying to regroup as I'd face my commute home to an empty house. For a very long time, I drove to and from school and everywhere else in total silence. It would take some time before I could listen to music in the car.

Under the guise of a busy life, I often felt lost. Though I got together with friends and family and continued to play tennis and mah jongg, there were many times during that first year as a widow when staying home alone was all I could handle. I would hit the wall and go in retreat, exhausted from pushing myself. I actually *needed* to be alone, to rest, to absorb my emotions, my grief, and internalize the events of the day. I learned it was alright if I declined an invitation—to say no thank you, not today, not tonight - when it was just too hard to go out, requiring more energy than I had to spare.

The first year after Jay's passing was simply about survival. But I also came to realize that my sister had overlooked one other obvious reason from her list as to why I'd be okay. *Me!* Despite an unthinkable loss, I was still me. I was still me as a mother, me at work, still had my same smarts and sense of humor, and still had my same values and interests. I could be alone and still enjoy my own company. When I had that epiphany, I knew I wasn't just going to survive. I was going to find a way to move forward with me, myself, and I.

IT'S ANOTHER DAY OF SUN

I saw the movie La La Land six months after Jay died. It starts off with a fabulous opening number—a scene of traffic at a standstill on a Los Angeles highway that quickly erupts into everyone dancing on top of their cars under a bright California sun.

I took to the melody and lyrics of that song in a way that surprised me. I'd listen to it repeatedly for months—at the gym, when I took walks, even when I was home. It never failed to get me going and lift my spirits. I finally realized that the reason I couldn't get enough of the opening song is that it always made me think of Jay in so many ways.

I know he would have loved that movie. What I visualized was how Jay would have developed his own dance interpretation of the opening number. It has a terrific upbeat rhythm with lots of energy, and I could see him doing a really fast cha-cha around the kitchen island, swinging his arms and singing along. It always made me smile, think of Jay's silliness, his fun-loving nature, and some of the simple ways in which he could be playful and find sheer joy.

But there's another aspect to the song that brought out something else about Jay. It's the story of actors who dream of hitting it big, but every day face the reality of challenges. Yet, when the next morning rolls around, with resilience, they declare—to quote the song title—It's Another Day of Sun. It's another day of hope and opportunity.

I know Jay viewed life this way. He always looked on the bright side of things. He seized every day to gain the most out of life, never wasting a moment, making something happen, for himself, his family, his friends, and his coworkers. He found meaning and purpose in life. He gave back to others. He took pleasure in every activity he pursued.

I decided I would try to honor Jay's memory by telling myself each morning when I woke up: *It's Another Day of Sun*. It's another day—to appreciate life with a positive outlook and to live it to the fullest—for that attitude captures the essence of Jay and keeps him alive in my heart.

LIFE IS ABOUT ENJOYING THE RIDE

Years ago, a dear friend of mine gave Jay a birthday card that was perfect for him. It had a bicycle on the front with the caption *"Life is about enjoying the ride."* I never removed that card from the bookshelf in my home office, despite the awful irony that Jay's passing was from a bike accident. I think it's a good mantra by which to live.

In these recent years, I've worked on *living* and trying to embrace change. I took up bridge. It turned out to be a really enjoyable game, stretching my brain. It also gave me endless opportunities to take lessons and play online, which was particularly helpful during the pandemic. I felt really good about learning bridge because it made me proud of myself for pursuing something new, on my own, in my new life.

I went on several spontaneous solo overnights to New York, treating myself to an evening and matinee Broadway show, something I'd never done before. You can get really great seats, even at the last minute, when all you need is one! I simply found it easier to do something I knew I would enjoy for myself, by myself, rather than having to plan and coordinate with others.

I cut back on work by entering a phased retirement program, what I referred to as transitioning to full-time fun. Now, after three years of part-time teaching, I am ready for and happily anticipating full retirement at the end of this year.

Undoubtedly, taking on the new role of mother-in-law when my son got married, followed one year later by becoming MomMom to my adorable grandson, were both joyous life-changing events. But the emotional challenges of adjusting to a shifting family dynamic without Jay are always present.

I continue to look for ways to enjoy the ride. However, I've also had to remind myself that even if Jay were here with me, there would still be some days that are harder than others, where the ride gets bumpy. I'd still have some worries, some disappointments, some fears. Life has its ups and downs, whether navigating it with a partner or alone as a widow.

HOPE IS WHEN YOU HEAR MUSIC IN THE FUTURE. FAITH IS WHEN YOU DANCE TO IT NOW.

I had a very good New Year's Eve on December 31, 2020. It was the fifth time I would be ringing in the new year without Jay. I had returned from visiting my kids in New York and was tired. But what should I do to fill the night? With nothing of interest on TV, I turned on Pandora on my iPad to listen to the 60s, 70s, and 80s station and played bridge online. I was surprised at how content I was to pass the time in this way.

But also, what surprised me was how my evening activity evolved. There were a lot of songs that came on with great beats, and I found myself tapping my feet with an increasing urge to dance. I finally couldn't resist it—and so each time, when a great song was played, I stepped into my foyer, set down my iPad, and danced—alone—in front of the mirror. I was my own dance partner, and I was fine with it! It was reminiscent of my childhood when I had done the very same thing behind my locked bedroom door.

In my mind, I felt like this was a pivot point, like I was on the precipice of some positive change. I've always loved music and dancing, and on that night, I was able to sing, dance, move and feel alive, even though I was alone. More importantly, I didn't know at the start of the night where it would lead, and yet there I was, laughing at myself and smiling. Life was full of possibilities.

#YOU WILL BE FOUND

It took me three years before I thought I might be ready to try dating, but my timing was off—the pandemic hit. So it took more than another year after that before I dipped my big toe into the dating sites.

It was slow going and very uninspiring! I was selective when I'd respond to messages and then would talk on the phone. The next step was insisting on a Zoom conversation before meeting anyone in person. Most of these experiences were not particularly fulfilling, but I needed to find myself again and awaken the part of me that went dormant from these years of living alone. I needed reminding that I was still capable of being good company and carrying on a witty conversation with a man I didn't know. Mostly, the handful of dates I had gave me entertaining anecdotes to share with my kids and friends, but absolutely no prospects.

Then something rather unexpected happened. Through a fluke encounter, I met someone I actually liked. We connected, having gone to the same high school and synagogue, sharing a love of the beach and shore, sharing similar values and closeness to our families. It felt easy and comfortable. He, too, had lost his spouse.

While I don't know where this will lead, it's still rolling along, and I am going with the flow. Sometimes it feels I am now on a dual journey. I have the disbelief that Jay is not here coupled with the disbelief that I've met someone. I've had fleeting feelings of betrayal and even survivor's guilt, neither of which I anticipated. I miss Jay so much and continue to cry that he is missing out on life, our life. I will always love Jay, *forever and ever*, but I can open and expand my heart to let someone else in. Who thought that would ever be possible?

Perhaps that is the biggest change in the way I now approach life. I really can't predict what will happen in the future. Good things can be right around the corner; life can change on a dime. I have to strive to live in the moment, seize opportunities, deal with whatever life hands me and make the best of it.

And so it goes—my journey of widowhood continues.

ABOUT THE AUTHOR

Cindy K. has been a college professor and resides in the suburbs of Philadelphia. She is the proud mother of a son and daughter, both of whom are wonderful, accomplished, and sensitive individuals. They have been a tremendous support to her on this journey. A terrific daughter-in-law and a beautiful grandson have enriched her life. Her email address is: cincin210821@gmail.com

It's a challenge
Trying to stay positive
Through this new normal

I am always in bed
Not sure how I can go on
It caught me off guard

Zoom zoom zoom away
Feelings are finding their way
Growing taking hold

Trying to pinpoint
What's my biggest obstacle
So I can fix it

Be gentle to you
Trust the process of your life
You are born to love

Stop thinking and jump
A whole big world is waiting
Just take that big plunge

GIRLS CAN WE TALK?!!

❧

WHAT HAPPENS TO US AFTER THE "THRILL" IS GONE?!!

BEBE NETTER SCHWARTZ

By some strange coincidence of acquaintances, a short few months after my loving husband of 40 years suddenly left my side and our loving marital bed, I met a very handsome man; inviting perfect teeth, smile, hair coiffed just so, strong athletic build, looks good enough to make me look better when we were together. Did I mention a well-dressed, pressed shirt, former lifeguard, dancer, and a motorcycle driver like my husband, not a 'Harley,' though? Funny thing, after my husband died, I pulled myself together and sojourned to Mexico for a month. On one of those sunny February days, outside a little beach town boutique, I came upon a sign that read:

"She dreams of mermaids, motorcycles, and meeting a man who can dance."

That sign made me emotional at the time, knowing my husband had been just that. This was February, and by summer's end, this motorcycle driving, dancing, beach man was magically standing in front of me! He had turned up in the flesh! Standing right in front of me, asking me to dance. The first words he ever said to me, "Do you want to dance?" Just like the song.

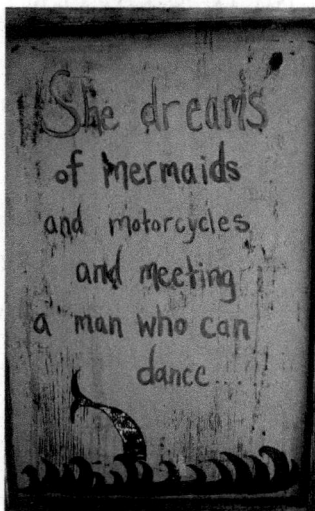

Well, I was in infatuation heaven! Like a schoolgirl, I looked at him with dreamy, wanting eyes. I knew I NEEDED this man! To pick me up, make me whole again, make me smile, and give me something to remind me I was still alive. I was silly and oh so needy! Did I say needy? It bears repeating. Here, take away my pain. You fill in the gaps. You tell me who I am and who I am supposed to be. I didn't know any better than that eight years ago. I knew nothing of who I was. I only knew I was sad, sorrowful, grieving for my deceased love and lover. Here was this man's task. Make everything "all better" for me and do it RIGHT NOW!!

And did he? Oh, he tried to be it all, do it all. Yes - our chemical attraction was 50 shades of just right, and yet something, someone was missing. Guess who it was? It was me!!! How was I ever going to relate to another man in an authentic, caring, supportive way if I had no clue who I was in the relationship we had begun to develop. And I had not a clue how to start and how to begin to find me.

We argued. We split up. We got back together, and life was serene again.

We argued. We split up. We got back together. Life was kind of serene.

Every time I came to an impasse with him, I threw him out! I was totally unable to see my part in any argument or discord. I must say he is the kind of guy that tends to be tough on himself, judgmental and critical of himself, and hates to make mistakes. Well, I have been a perfectionist too. I just was unable to see it in myself. There was no meeting of the minds or damaged psyches. No talking it out together. Easier to tell him to leave than to look at myself. Yes, I talked it out with my closest confidantes who, of course, told me what I wanted to hear. Then finally, the best therapist helped me to "see." Open my heart and see.

Every time it was definitely over between us, I forced myself to see my part in the breakup. I became introspective. I made certain to spend time by myself. I had never spent time alone in my whole married life. It was really tough and challenging turning so deeply inward. I journaled. I meditated. Then after a few weeks, I would begin to miss him, and before long, there he was once again, willing to start anew.

Each time we broke up, I went deep into my soul and asked myself, "Who are you? Who are you really? What are you going to do for the rest of your life? What is your intention for being here on earth? Being a member of the greater human community?" I dove deep within myself. Participated in spiritual retreats, mindful meditation talks and courses, and continued weekly therapy sessions. What was my purpose? What was my true purpose?

Then it all started to make sense to me. Who I had always been all along, just never having the opportunity and courage to reach out and BE me! A wife, a mother, a daughter, a sister, eventually a "GramBe." Roles I happily played. Now it was time to really see and truly know the full potential of my existence. And I did! I learned I am a resilient, strong, generous, loyal, fun, supportive, committed, and loving woman. A woman who lives in the present moment without judgment or expectations and who truly knows just who she truly is!

So back to the handsome man. Well, he is still here. It ain't always perfect or even pretty, though he still is. I have accepted this man as a human being separate from me and so different from my dearest husband. The comparisons were never made—just known. I see who this man is in my life and the purpose that he serves in it. A caring, giving man who will do just about anything to see me happy. Yeh, he still has his moods and takes life pretty seriously sometimes. And me, I live my own story and learned his story is his and mine is mine. When there is an issue between us, I do my best to remember to breathe and let it go. Well, he is here, and I am here too. It is ok. I am ok. We are ok together. I am learning to let it go and bring it in at the same time. I learned to change my mind. I certainly cannot change anyone else's! My heart is forever entwined with my dearest hubby and presently connected to this good, sturdy man. How lucky am I!

Finally, I know who I am! Without losing my husband, without being a widow, and being on my own, I doubt I would have gained the insight and wisdom I have found within. Without the reflection in the mirror that my new partner held up to me, I do not think my life would forever be my own. That mirror provided me the opportunity to really see who was there reflecting back at me. Gratefully I finally saw ME! Perfect in all my imperfections! And back to the thrill? Well, it's not gone. It's there and can be thrillingly coaxed when the mood strikes. The best part is I no longer NEED the thrill from anyone else. I am the thrill! And so it is...

NOW I KNOW I'M STRONG
NOW I KNOW I AM WORTHY
NOW I AM ENOUGH

AND THEN THERE'S THE "CHILDREN"

On the last day of August, 2013, my most loving and genius father died within a week of having a stroke. His zest and zeal for life was so strong, he was certain to be the last human standing at the end of time. The very next morning, my husband of 40 years announced he was having a heart attack and within three weeks he was gone too. These two vital men, as close as any father and son, are gone, at least from this plain. Both of these wonderful and strong men dying within a few weeks of each other was devastating not only to me, the daughter and widow, but also to the children. the grandchildren. These two outstanding dominant male figures so present in the lives of my son and my daughter, suddenly ceased to exist. I remember falling to my knees in the hospital crying over and over, "My daughter! My little girl! She's just a little girl!" To live the remainder of her life without the love and guidance, wisdom, and creativity of her Daddy and Pop-pop. She was just out of college, living on her own, finishing graduate school out of the area. How very sad! And my son, the older of the two children, very close to his Pop-pop and Dad. So many adventures and fun times together. Over! Just over! Just like that! My son was newly engaged to the most outstanding, young woman. We were all happy and excited to experience the next steps in their lives. Now this journey was to be made alone, without them by our sides.

My dearest little daughter, in her early 20's had suddenly lost her main guide, and sounding board, her father. He was not there to listen to her ideas for the future. No more almost too tight embracing bear hugs. No more sidecar rides on the motorcycle to get ice cream, or take a quick trip to Maine.

My dearest son, left without the huge personality of his so smart and self-made father. The jokester, the comic, the man who loved his children so much, showed it, wanted his children to do it all, have it all, see it all, was gone.

I was so deep in my own grief and loss. I think literally being in shock, I turned to these little souls to comfort and support me. And they did. Somehow for the love of their mother and the loving memory of their father, they managed to set aside their own pain and disbelief and become present for me, the sorrowful widow.

So how did they do it you may want to know? First, the little girl stood in front of the overflowing congregation at Rodeph Shalom in Philadelphia, where her parents, grandparents, and great-grandparents were married. Gathering her thoughts and moving with grace and ease to the pulpit, she gave the eulogy for her dearest Daddy. With a strong, unwavering voice she spoke words of solace, humor, love and wisdom beyond her years. As a grieving widow and her mother, I was awed and smiled with pride through my tears.

My son had a band, still has the band and had a "show" already scheduled and set up at a local spot in town. The show must go on! was the motto that late September. And it did! My children packed the house with family, friends, fans, food, booze, music, laughter, tears, and memories! There were hugs and strength and caring support that night. This loving community gathered around and cocooned us. This was the exact memorial both the Pop-pop and the Dad would have loved.

It was from that moment we collectively moved forward with the knowledge of how much we were loved and supported and the knowledge we always had each other to turn towards when we felt weak or needed that extra push to go on.

The little girl moved on with her life achieving her master's degree. What inner iron she must have had along with tenacity and ambition remembering how very much she was loved and nurtured by her Dad. Knowing the pain her Mommy was experiencing, she encouraged me to come and visit her and explore the thriving Brooklyn where she was living. Her intention I believe, was to assure herself I was functioning and to share some of the city's vibrancy with me. The little girl wanted to give her Mom reasons to smile. She opened her life to me, friends, work, exciting Brooklyn boutiques, restaurants, concerts, even teaching me to utilize the subway. This sweet, wise little girl set aside her own pain and grief even as she continued to work and experience the start of her own new relationship. All in order to support and care for her Mom.

The older child, the boy, happened to be living at my house with his fiancee. This was most fortunate and fortuitous. Because of my immense grief I was unable to do pretty much of anything. This young couple took on the management of the house, the marketing, the cooking, and the total care of our two dogs, one of which was only a scant three months old. I let them! I was not functioning enough to do anything else but let them! About a month or so later, the little boy found another way to move us forward. He, along with his exceptional and beautiful fiancee, decided to continue with their lives and began planning "The Best!" one-of-a-kind wedding in Sedona, Arizona. Overlooking the majestic setting of the red rocks, filled with their vortex of magic, at sunset, his sister, the little girl, with her brilliant and meaningful words was the officiant. 80 guests made the journey and participated in the overflowing love and joy of the wedding ceremony. The bride was stunning! The groom was handsome! Ever present were the spirits of their Pop-pop and their Father. All present felt this deeply, strongly, truly. A brilliant full moon rose that night over the outdoor reception festivities. We felt the moonbeams shining down on us with the devotion and satisfaction of the men who were deceased and yet very much participants. We danced with abandon. We rejoiced unbounded. We reveled and ate the best cakes ever!

I look at my children now, 8 years later and see their eyes filled with the deepest love, the deepest connection that we all hold for each other. The love we experience together is deep and strong held together by the forever spirits of the beloved Grandfather and the Father. We call it the "fullfam" bond. The little boy and his wife have two healthy and spirited little boys of their own. The little girl is now married to a loving, solid man. The fullfam live close to each other. Everyday that goes by we speak the Dad's name, my husband. More than that we include him in our thinking and doing. Keeping him in the present makes us smile. That's how he wants it.

We all experience the reality of this.

We all know it as fact.

We are blessed to live it.

And I the widow, the mother, the daughter am the luckiest one of all.

And so it is...

ONE DAY I JUST KNEW

One day I just knew
I awoke to my own goodness. My worth. My understanding.
I was enough
One day I just knew.
The lessons of my life, the beauty and the pain. The gifts and
the losses.
One day I just knew.
One day I just knew who I was.
One day I was aware.

The fear became known as only a thought.
I gave up the worry, the pain of the worry knowing it did
nothing to change my life or the outcome.
One day I just knew.
I knew grasping and clinging, wanting, and expectation
brought disappointment and suffering.
One day I just knew.
And it was so.

ABOUT THE AUTHOR

Bebe Netter Schwartz is a Philadelphia native. She has a positive, generous spirit. She is living a purposeful life which includes teaching fitness and mindfulness meditation. "Life can only be understood backwards; but it must be lived forwards." Soren Kierkegaard

To contact Bebe go to bebeschwartz@gmail.com

HAIKU THREADS

❦

JILL A. RUPINSKI

*E*ach of these three groups of writings are comprised of multiple haiku to be read as a short story. They are based on my experiences in the first days and months after my husband's passing.

AN INVISIBLE PRESENCE

The first time alone
Everyone left to go home
Quietly sitting.

A crushing silence
My mind was open and free
A spirit came in.

The soft ring of bells
Rhythmic and familiar
I knew he was there.

I turned to listen
Was it real or imagined?
An Invisible presence.

FROM THE OTHER SIDE

Many sleepless nights
From an anxious state of mind
A swift relief came.

I saw the winged form
Heard a bang at the window
From the other side.

I knew instantly
He came to say he was there
No more would I fret.

The unexpected
It is always around us
Do not be surprised.

THE SPIRIT KNOWS

The answer is there
Just let it into your life
Do not question it.

Confident and proud
A demonstrative being
This regal feline

She was sent to me
As a step for my healing
Giving me much joy.

She did not stay long
The spirit knows when it is time
Life's tasks completed.

Remember the good
And reject the broken heart
Wait for another.

My husband just died
I was there for his last breath
The nightmare begins

This is what I know
Can't keep going on like this
I must make a plan

Dream big is my goal
Senior citizen actress
Is my newest take

I am proud of me
Gaining peace strength and purpose
Friends show me the way

She believed she could
So she worked so very hard
And guess what? She did

Don't worry a lot
Go out and make those mistakes
Just learn the lesson

I AM HERE

❧

ROZ WEXLER

I was married for 50 years. Wow! I met my husband at a dance, and I liked him right away. We dated for a year, and then we became engaged for a year. When we married, I was a young 19 years old, and by the time I was 22, I had two children..! My husband was very low key and easy going, and I was the exact opposite! I was a dreamer. I imagined becoming a dancer, an actress, or a make-up artist. I loved people, and I always enjoyed their company. My husband always supported my dreams, and when my children were a little older, he pushed me to go to hairdressing school. Then I traveled to New York for classes in facials and make-up in order to get my license to be a professional.

Through the years, we traveled with the family, and when we traveled alone, my parents were happy to watch the children.

My husband was a romantic. We held hands all of the time, and our friends always mentioned they thought we were cute. One day our life changed when my husband and his friend were a victim of a crime that ended in the death of our friend. My husband was struck in the head and left for dead. The case was never solved. Our lives were never the same because we were traumatized and very depressed. He was unable to work and had to go on disability. Luckily I was able to use my degree by doing bridal make-up. I enjoyed being able to work with women at such a happy time in their lives.

My husband's health was complicated by a subnormal hematoma in his brain, which was being constantly monitored by the doctors. At the end of March 2012, we were home watching TV. He had a sudden problem with his hand. We went to the hospital, and he had surgery the next morning, which caused him to have a seizure and a stroke in recovery. I never had the chance to talk with him, and he passed away five days later. My children never came to the hospital or to see him, and to this day, I never heard from them again. I drove home by myself to an empty apartment with no one to hold me or to comfort me. I was not used to being alone, so I went to a mall near me. I went to the top floor and looked over the railing with thoughts of jumping. Of course I didn't. I was depressed, not crazy!

So here I am 10 years later. I'm standing and moving forward. I was lucky enough to have found friends that are widows, and they understand and support me in many ways. My cousins came to me when they found out my husband had died. They continue to be part of my life. I still have my sense of humor, and it really helps. I enjoy it when I make people laugh.

When I look back over my life, I think of how I was as a child. I always made sure I looked my best, and I always enjoyed the friends in my life. I think these traits have given me direction and strength. My aunt, who is now 100, sold make-up in a high- end department store. When I think of her, I know she really added so much to my life. I went to her house when I was young, and she would show me her make-up, and I was fascinated by it. Her influence helped shape my career.

When I think of my life, I realize I am stronger than I give myself credit for. It took a long time to get here, but I'm here!

INTRODUCING ME

SUSAN J. GROSS

WHO AM I?

*a*t 79, I am trying to find out who I am. I lost my husband when I was 60, and I know I've come a long way, but I'm still working on spreading the word and helping others heal and join the world again. Luckily I kept notes in a journal so I thought I'd share interesting and challenging experiences that I've had along the way. Some of the entries are during our marriage, and some are after my husband's passing. I hope you may be able to relate, and they might be helpful. So here we go...

WEATHERING THE STORMS

When your younger self is making plans for your life, you get the feeling that you are totally in control of everything. You know there will be challenges, but there's a feeling you will have choices and many possibilities. You don't predict loss and devastation. If you're lucky, this smooth or slightly bumpy sailing goes on for an indefinite number of years. I've had significant bumps, but because of positive attitudes and the support of a dedicated spouse, we were able to weather the storms. It wasn't easy, but when I look back, I marvel at our strength.

BORING CAN BE GOOD

It seems like at least five lifetimes ago that life was somewhat "normal" or "boring" as I like to put it. Boring is very good! To me, it means things are quiet and under control with no major surprises and an enormous level of gratitude for health and safety. What could be better than that? But in 2003, my strength was tested to the limit. My 41-year marriage and our 46-year partnership came to a crashing end! Widowhood has taken me to another level. When you lose your frame of reference, and you realize life's challenges are totally your responsibility, and you try to keep up with this impossible task. But how do you do that when you can't get out of bed, you can't stop crying, and you can't think straight? From my experience, the only solution is to go with the flow, Bathe in the sadness and reach the lowest point possible. Indulge yourself and feel the hurt. Get it out of your system. I always felt crying keeps your heart soft, so I submerged myself in tears. It was always my goal to never be bitter but to keep the love inside always.

FINDING MY HUSBAND

I have a story
Young teen meets a boy at a dance
Starts a life of love.

I grew up in the city of Philadelphia, and about six blocks from my house was the Felton Movie theatre. I would regularly go on Saturdays. One Saturday, my life unexpectedly changed when I got to see Marlon Brando on the big screen in Guys and Dolls. I was in heaven! I returned a number of times just to drool and watch him on the screen. When I met my husband at 14, he had the Marlon Brando aura, I was gone!

I know you are wondering where this is going, but after my husband passed, I took a poetry writing class, and here is the result:

Marlon—May I call you that?

I hope it isn't too informal. If you want, I will call you Mr. Brando.

You have no reason to know me. I am a 70-year-old fan of yours who was given an assignment in a poetry class to write a piece inspired by art. We were sent to the adjoining library to find a piece of art that appealed to us. Roaming the art section, I happened to see a book of Great Life Magazine Photographs. By divine intervention, I opened the book randomly to page 306, and there was a picture of you and your sister Jocelyn from 1948. My heart skipped a beat, and suddenly I realized that I needed to thank you for a lifetime of happiness. I wrote this poem for you.

Little Susan Bernstein in the Felton Movie Theater paid 10 cents for admission on a Saturday to see Guys and Dolls. Slick gambler Sky Masterson lit up the screen.

Gene Simmons was Mission Girl Sister Sarah Brown, the ultimate good girl—like me.

The earth shook big time.

OMG, transformed and breathless, I was hooked.

Saw the movie over and over and compared all the boys I met to you and NO ONE CAME CLOSE!

Until at 14, I **accidentally** met my future husband—and we married just like you and Sister Sarah.

He had great clothes, style, attitude, face, cool—the works —INSTANT!

A lifetime later, you and my Sky Masterson are both gone, but.......

Watching the DVD of Guys and Dolls is my salvation!!!!

THANK YOU THANK YOU

KEEPING UP WITH THE TIMES: USING MY VOICE

It's a Sunday morning at about 9 A.M., and the year is 1972. My husband of 11 years is about to walk our adorable and energetic terrier, Vickie. As he is leaving the house, for some reason, he turns to me and casually says, "when I come back, I'll have scrambled eggs, and I don't want them brown." I know it's 1973, and women are supposed to handle everything—work—house—children—but you don't want your eggs brown? I innocently asked to confirm the request! "YOU DON'T WANT THEM BROWN?" He confirmed the request and left for the important walk. This was the first I'd heard mention of eggs being brown. "You've got to be kidding me," ran through my soul. So 15 minutes later, when sir Alan returned to our abode, the Stepford Wife had his scrambled eggs warm and ready to enjoy. Oh, by the way, they weren't brown—they were bright green! Yes, they were bright green because, luckily, I had food coloring in the house!

That was me. It's hard to believe that it was almost 50 years ago. I was just 30, and I know that simple act on a Sunday morning was a major turning point in my life. You see, because of circumstances and, of course, unconscious choices, I had been a caregiver all of my childhood. We met when we were very young and married young, so I had no time to give up my caregiving role. But for some reason, at 30, I had the desire to be done with it. I had missed the women's movement because I was responsible for children and I was working. That special Sunday morning was "**MY PERSONAL WOMEN'S MOVEMENT!**" When Prince Charming announced he couldn't eat them—I reminded him they weren't brown, and I left the room.

THERE WERE NO TV CAMERAS OR PARADES FOR MY WOMEN'S MOVEMENT....

JUST ME, and IT WAS LIFE ALTERING!

HUMOR IN SADNESS

And now it's time that you get a taste of Alan's personality. He was in chronic pain for at least ten years, and his life kept getting smaller and smaller. He couldn't work at what he loved, and he couldn't walk, but this is a comment he made when we were sitting outside the house eating breakfast on a relaxing summer day. "**It's lucky I'm not dating,**" says my dear sweet husband of 40 years as he sits in his motorized scooter taking a huge assortment of medications while wincing because of chronic pain. How horrible to watch someone you love continue to lose abilities as he nobly tries to keep his dignity through humor. "**You just have to learn**

to love your pain," he says. I'm in awe of his courage!

NEW SET OF RULES

Luck ran out on July 25th, 2003, when I became a widow, and I had to learn a whole new set of rules. But where do you find the rules?

"There are 300-page books on widowhood, but who can concentrate that long and all these rules don't apply to everyone."

But lucky me—by chance, when I was in Cape May, a book finally caught my attention because it had the word laugh in the title. I vaguely remember laughing. I thought. The title was "I'd Rather Laugh," written by Linda Richman. She lost her son and also became non-functioning. I could truly relate. She was housebound for over a year, and at her lowest point, she finally decided to leave her New York apartment and visit her religious leader for much needed rescue and direction. She unloaded her entire story and was eager for words of comfort and strength but what she heard was, "I can't even imagine!" She was sure she heard wrong. Where's my comfort and solution? But instead, she said, "For this, I schlepped on three buses?"

That was it! That was my cure. I laughed and knew whatever was going to happen had to depend on me! No more poor me. I was going to reach out and find myself. I found a good therapist and joined a support group. I will explain about the support group a little later. I'd like to share some other experiences before that—stay tuned!!!

SPEAKING TRUTH SO YOU DON'T FEEL LIKE YOU ARE CRAZY

Well, here I am, a total non-functioning mess, which is totally new to me. I've always been active in the world, with my friends, family, and career. How am I supposed to know how to deal with this new catatonic me? A lifetime love affair was taken away. My husband and I met when we were only 14 and 16. We literally grew up together, and we married when we were still innocent babes at 19 and 21. But somehow, we knew how to love and deal with life together.

HERE'S MY FIRST WIDOW EXPERIENCE CALLED, I THINK I SHOCKED THE FUNERAL DIRECTOR

It just happened. If you've been unlucky enough to have to plan a funeral, you'll know what I am talking about. You are taken into a large room at the height of your sadness and confusion and asked to choose a casket out of an extremely large inventory. Your emotions are raw, unending tears, and the desire to just crawl in a hole and hide—but decisions have to be made. Imy fragile state, I said to the funeral director, "do you have any that are beachy?" He looked at me in confusion, but it made perfect sense to me. My husband and I loved the beach, and it really defined our entire life. His final career was spent photographing the beach, so I felt it should be his forever environment. He hesitated and then brought me to a natural washed wood casket which was perfect. When that was settled, I gave him my husband's Bloomingdales charge card to put in his jacket pocket in case he needed it. I didn't need to explain that it was his favorite store. He just thanked me. I'M SURE HE'LL REMEMBER ME!

THE EMOTIONAL CAR SAGA

Today I had to go to the car dealership to trade in our van. The Chrysler van meant a lot to Alan and I. It was a working and traveling family vehicle. Alan was a fine art photographer, and he did art shows all over the east coast. He would prepare his work for the shows and then pack up the van to the brim with all of his beautiful photographs, and off he would go. We also used the van for wonderful family vacations, and we were able to take so many possessions because of its incredible amount of space. I also loved driving the van because it really made me feel tall and important on the road. The extra emotional attachment came near the end of our ownership when we had to get a handicapped license plate to accommodate Alan's failing health. After he passed, and I didn't have a need anymore for the van, I knew I had to say goodbye to it and its memories. I didn't have anyone available that day to come with me to the dealership, so I gathered up my strength and went alone. I was fine on the way over, but when the extremely sweet young salesman came over and I had to explain my needs, I started to cry. Of course I cried most of the time I was in the showroom, but because of his warm personality, he was able to help me trade the van and get a smaller car just for myself. When I told him I would get the new car the next day because my daughter would come with me, he understood how painful it was for me to leave the van there. He told me to wait outside while he cleaned the van out, and he made the transfer without my involvement at all. Within about 45 minutes, the switch was completed, and I drove out of the dealership without the Chrysler. I managed to survive—thanks to the kindness of a random salesman.

FRANK & I HAVE ALWAYS HAD A THING

I've always loved Frank Sinatra, but now I love him even more. I was driving one Sunday morning, and on the radio, the hosts were singing Happy Birthday to Frank. Wow!!! I realized our birthdays are a week apart! An extra great connection. Of course I started to analyze the coincidence.

Then they played his song, I Got The World on a String Sitting on a Rainbow, and then came the line...

Life's a beautiful thing as long as I hold the string. THAT'S IT...

It gave me new insight into widowhood and moving forward!!!! The string represents stability, and in this stage, we let go temporarily, and the goal is to grab hold of it again.

Then crazy enough, they played the song, **How Do You Keep the Music Playing.**

And the words continue how do you make it last? How do you keep it from fading too fast?

INSIGHTFUL MOMENT!...... OUR BIGGEST CHALLENGE.....

KEEPING THE MUSIC AND LOVE ALIVE......

THANKS FRANK!!!! LOVE YOU!!!!!

I'M UP FOR THE CHALLENGE!

ABOUT THE AUTHOR

Susan J Gross has spent her entire life learning to implement positivity and strength. She is a retired Philadelphia career teacher who spent over 33 years motivating and exposing students to the world outside of the box. She always focused on how creativity and openness can be life-changing. Her main goal was always to raise self-esteem and self-acceptance in every student.

When her lifelong boyfriend and husband passed away in 2003, she could not continue as she was, and she had to retire. After working very hard to regain balance, she got her spark back. Susan decided to use her experiences to motivate and enhance the lives of other widows. She is putting her passions to work, helping other widows find strength, passion, and laughter.

Susan has two wonderful children, a great son-in-law, and two fabulous grandchildren.

Books

www.amazon.com/Someone-Used-Love-Me-positive/
www.amazon.com/Think-Turned-Corner-Someone-Used/

INVISIBLE WIDOW

CAROL SALOMON

*H*ow I remember THAT Autumn day in 2018! The day that changed my life!

For over twenty years, my husband had extensive medical issues. Our weekly visits to different specialists were our main activity. He looked forward to these visits as he always had delightful edible treats for each doctor. Everyone knew him! The medical staff became our community. One administrator even presented my husband with a flag that flew over the United States Air Force Memorial!

Then, suddenly these complicated and stressful—and yes, social—appointments ended. He passed away on THAT Autumn day in 2018.

Friends and family gathered after the traditional funeral at a luncheon. They checked in for a while. Then nothing.

My loneliness that followed during the next few weeks led me to a quiet, desolate space. My friends from every one of my life stages stopped contacting me. Relatives and co-workers were too busy to send a text or email. Did anyone at all remember me? I shared my plea for human connection with one of my favorite doctors. She said I had a new title—namely the "invisible widow"!

I was no longer a part of a couple. I was a single woman. People did not know what to say to me nor what they could do for me.

A few weeks passed, and slowly these humans began to reconnect with me. I started to revitalize despite the loss.

Snow White (from the Brothers Grimm) said, "It is when we are most lost that we sometimes find our truest friends."

As I try to keep my balance and move along (as Albert Einstein suggested in this quote, "Life is like riding a bicycle, to keep your balance, you must keep moving.") my mind concentrated on deep, loving memories. I found myself enjoying the sunshine, smiles, and new and old adventures.

However, I did find myself in a bewildering situation one cloudy afternoon. Unbelievable to my own ears, I heard myself shout aloud.... "I see a ghost!"

It was the outline of a friendly person inside the frame of a bedroom door. It was an eerie lifelike vision! I froze in amazement and checked out this spiritual visitor. Just as I was called the "invisible widow" I now seemed to enter the world of the supernatural. I was not frightened but seemed to enjoy the fact that my husband stopped by to make sure that I was safe and secure in my new apartment. Thank you, Sal, for visiting me!

"It is only with the heart that one can see rightly; what is essential is INVISIBLE to the eye."

- Antoine de Saint-Expuery, The Little Prince.

ABOUT THE AUTHOR:

Carol attended Temple University. She has a Master's Degree in Early Childhood Education. Carol has worked with children at schools, camps, museums and art centers.

Carol continues to teach preschool and has been a widow since October 2018.

Life can be simple
Pay attention to the now
Moment by moment

Angers tears and fears
Live where you were but I see
You live in my heart

Women are soft rocks
Strength covered with cushioning
To hold our friends up

Friends carry me through
When not busy with husbands
Our group is a gift

The new me now reads
No more reading self help books
So I'm not perfect

Getting through the day
Pushing myself back to life
It's a slow process

MOVING FORWARD, ONE DAY AT A TIME

KAREN CORNELL

I was leaving my daughter's apartment in New York City, where I visit my sweet 22-month-old grandson (Noah) every other weekend and watching the colorful autumn leaves flutter by the window. I started to think that this must be a sign, a message—as the seasons are changing, now must be the time for me to move ahead with changes in my life.

Noah has turned into the joy of my life, especially since my husband (Neal) passed away suddenly five years ago. To compound the sadness, my mother passed away two years ago, and I lost my brother this past year. My husband was my rock, and my mother was my best friend for the entire 65 years of my life. This great loss left me feeling untethered and on shaky ground. I soon realized that I had to learn to listen to myself for answers to my questions, with no one else who could read my thoughts or understand what is right for me. This was the first time in my adult life that I had to focus on myself. This was very hard because I was always focused on my husband, my mother, who was a widow for 30 years, and my children. There just wasn't the time for me to stop and think of what was best for me. I was raising two children, working full time, keeping on top of the household and errands, and making sure that Mom's needs were met. Life was the 49-yard dash—how much yardage can I complete in a 24-hour day.

Now, I see the time passing quickly, just as the leaves are blowing away in the wind. There are more years behind me than ahead of me. What should I do at this stage of my life? I work full-time as an event planner at a university in the city. I've been there 24 years and still enjoy my job. I moved from the suburbs to the city when Neal died. I ran away from home. I couldn't bear to remain in the neighborhood where we did everything together. I would see Neal in my mind, walking down the street to meet me for dinner, wearing his long, warm winter coat with a silly smile on his face. He was always acting silly and up for a good laugh. His sweet smile went right through me like a coat surrounding me with his warmth. I thought the city would dull the past and the pain, but it just served as a distraction. I would run around all day with work and attend events in the evening, so I wouldn't have to go home and be alone. I made new friends, single women, of course—I am no longer part of a couple, and therefore I am relegated to the role of a single woman. Most of my friends and family who are couples saw me once after Neal died, and that was that.

After five years in the city and living through the challenges of Covid, I am now planning to move back to the suburbs. My mother left me her condo, and I am renovating it with plans to move back to the country in the spring. My children said I should sell the condo and buy something new, but this was my mother's home for 30 years, and now it feels like my home. I want the quiet now, in a clean neighborhood with minimal crime, and I want to be surrounded by the peacefulness of nature. I want space, not just a small apartment, where my grandson can visit and run across the room and ride a scooter outside on the street. This is my decision. I had to think hard to decide what was best for me— I think this is it. I surely hope so.

I want to retire. I want to travel and see the world. I want to visit new cities and new cultures and experience new environments. I can still walk for long periods of time, I am still lucid, and I can hold my end of a conversation. I can still make plans, follow up on the logistics, and take care of myself for those unexpected events that will undoubtedly occur. I am still healthy and well, but for how much longer? My husband died suddenly, and it scares me that I can die suddenly too, and then I won't be here to help take care of my children. They lost their father unexpectedly, and I try to be both father and mother to them—offering advice, helping with their financial burdens when I can, assisting with major life decisions. My son is getting married next spring—I am scared that I will cry throughout the entire ceremony and reception, dwelling on the fact that my husband is not here to see his son married. Neal was my son's best friend, and he is missing out on so much in our lives, but all we can do is hold him in our hearts and think of him during these special moments.

I want to spend more time with my grandson Noah who is my sunshine – he lights up my life with his sweet smile, his head of golden curls, his belly laughs, his silly antics, and his chatter. I drink him up like a wellness tonic. When I left him last weekend in NY, Noah cried when I walked out the door, and so did I. I was anticipating going back to my apartment with no one to greet me when I walked through the door, and Noah was missing his playmate, who focuses only on him when I visit for long weekends. His parents are both busy with their demanding careers, but I have the time to sit with Noah. We read books, play with his cars and trains, look out the window and wave to the buses passing by, sing songs, and play silly games like "Where is Noah" and "Peek-a-Boo." Neal would have loved Noah—now I love Noah for the both of us.

Noah will grow up quickly. He will go to school, play with his friends and participate in after school activities. Noah needs his grandma now, and I need my Noah. I am fascinated by his growth and development. There are so many changes when I see him every two weeks. I am watching him develop from a baby into a precocious toddler. Every time I see him, I say, "Noah, you are all grown up now. When did this happen." And his face lights up when he sees me. When my daughter and son were born, my mother used to say, "This child touches my heart." Now, I understand—my Noah touches my heart.

My mother never met Noah, but she knew that Morgan was pregnant. I used to say to Mom that Morgan wanted me to take an apartment in NY, and my mother would say, "What's the big deal!" Maybe when I retire, I can keep my condo in the suburbs near my son and a small apartment in NY near my daughter and her family.

When I listen to myself, I hear my mother's voice and my husband's thoughts. They are part of me now. My mother used to say that we have one heart, and I know now that she and Neal are part of my heart and they will live within me forever.

I don't know if I am making the right decisions in my life, but Neal used to say to me, "If you don't make a decision, then the decision is made for you." I am lucky to have been loved in my life. Now, it's time to for me to share the love that I have left with my grandson, my children, my family, and friends, and give it away.

Epitaph by Merrit Malloy

"...Love doesn't die,

People do.

So, when all that's left of me

Is love,

Give me away."

MY JOURNEY

❧

CINDY GRODANZ

*M*y husband Robbie passed away on February 17, 2019, at the age of 69. He had Parkinson's for 12 years, and I was his care partner. I was a professor at the Community College for over 20 years and had recently retired.

I loved my husband so much. We had a 50-year relationship and were married for 47 years, a real love match. When he died, I was devastated, but I knew that his suffering had ended. Now it was time to comfort my four children and their families and go on with my new normal.

I had to deal with the loneliness and the quiet. It was time to tap into my inner strength. My mother had been left a widow at 49 and had four children to raise. She was a strong woman and never complained. I took my strength from her. I was a 69-year-old with just a dog.

I was coping pretty well with my situation and looking for new ways to spend time. Then Covid hit. I turned to old hobbies and some new ones: puzzles, piano, reading, canasta, walking, and even tap dancing. Really anything to keep me active.

The support of my wonderful children and my friends has been so important. I consider myself to be very fortunate to have all this love in my life. I have always been an upbeat person. I enjoy my life, and I deserve it.

GETTING IT

When a woman becomes a widow, there are many people who want to help and comfort her. These friends and family are wonderful, but they may not get it. They just really cannot identify with your situation.

The couples that you and your husband had as friends will feel very upset and will want to help you. Many of these relationships will fade because we seem to live in a couple's world. Your divorced friends want to be there for you, but they are in a very different emotional situation, being that you are still in love with your husband.

Your children are also grieving, and they have their own lives to live. They, too, cannot get that you miss the relationship you had, especially the intimacy, as well as the companionship.

In general, the only people who "get it" are other widows. Of course, they are not the same, either. Everyone grieves in their own way.

Other widows get what it's like to lie in bed alone. Other widows get what it's like to give away their husband's clothes. Other widows get what it's like to see couples walking hand-in-hand along the beach. Other widows get what it's like to see a "sign" like a cardinal or a butterfly and think it's a message. Other widows get what it's like to eat dinner alone, watch television, and then climb into bed.

Other widows can help you move forward. We've been there. We went through it, and we are in it. We have our own stories. We are strong women. We will go on.

IT'S ALL RIGHT, AND IT'S ALL NORMAL

- Sleeping on his side of the bed
- Hugging a stuffed animal in bed
- Wearing his clothes
- Not cleaning out his closet
- Watching romantic movies, reading romance books, and tearing up Crying in the supermarket
- Putting his picture in every room of the house
- Staring at his picture and just remembering

- Dreaming about him
- Not dreaming about him
- Wearing your wedding rings
- Putting your rings away
- Making him into a saint
- Remembering his faults
- Missing your old life
- Starting your new life
- Being sad
- Being happy
- Worrying about money
- Spending money on yourself
- Feeling sorry for yourself
- Realizing that you can still be happy

MY 5-7-5'S

Life's like a puzzle
Searching for the perfect piece
To find your true love

We needed more time
To love, to laugh. to grow old
God had other plans

Reading lots of books
Learning more about myself
Questioning my life

My life does go on
Getting up to face the day
It's my new normal

We still have a life
After rain we see rainbows
You will find your peace

Middle of the night
Loneliness overwhelms me
I am lost in thoughts

He was my person
Do you believe in angels?
Everlasting love

It's not how we die
It's how we lived in this life
He knew he was loved

I feel my power
When my friends hold the mirror
And shine it on me

My dog has one eye
Yet he is happy each day
He's a good teacher

Just hear the music
Long as we are singing our song
The love keeps flowing

A cloud hangs over
Sometimes heavy rain pours down
Most days sun shines through

I am a new me
Stepping out of my comfort
Looking for a change

Be always grateful
No matter what may happen
It will keep you safe

MY JOURNEY INTO THE UNKNOWN

❦

I. BROWN

*I*t was a beautiful Memorial Day weekend at the Jersey shore. One of the first perfect weather Memorial Days in a number of years. As we sat on the porch, enjoying the warm weather and our neighbors, my husband announced that this was going to be a great summer! As the saying goes, "Man plans and God laughs" his premonition was not to come true. On June 18th, 2016, after two difficult weeks in the hospital, my love took his last breath. I sat by his side in utter disbelief. When you experience the loss of a spouse, it feels like your world has come to an end. Whether it is a sudden death or after a prolonged illness, death shocks your system and clouds your reality.

In the summer of 1976, I was introduced to Bernie, and my love story began. We married in 1977, blended our families, and moved into our new home. I was a wife and mother with him at my side to love, care for and protect us. I still live in the same house, unable to bear the thought of living in a house I never shared with him.

Our health survived four separate diagnoses of cancer and a total of eight separate treatments over the course of 39 years. We filled those years with work, travel, theater, and family occasions and purchased a second home at the beach in Margate, NJ. I honestly think that the beach house helped keep him young. When we went over the bridge, he would get this big grin because he was going on vacation. There now stands a bench dedicated in his memory atop the dune at our beach entrance. He has an unobstructed view of the ocean forever.

He never admitted to being sick or complained of pain. While he may have fooled himself, he certainly fooled me. My reading material moved from fiction to medical journal articles regarding new treatments and procedures that might prolong his life. I worried, but fooled myself into thinking we had many years left together. I thought we would grow old together. Instead, I am just growing old.

Being Jewish, we observed Shiva for seven days. That period of time was unreal. Our home was filled with family and friends. The family took turns staying overnight so I would not be alone. We shared stories long into the night and learned so many new things about each other. At the end of the week, when things went back to the "new normal", I realized I was a widow and alone. What a horrible realization!

Those who think there is a

time limit when grieving have

never lost a piece of their heart

-- Donna Ashworth

I was lost. My children and grandchild were/are wonderful and supportive. I am blessed to have them. They did everything possible to fill part of my void, but at the end of the day, I was alone and sad. My friends have never abandoned me, always including me in their plans. It felt like overnight, I went from a strong, competent woman to a shell of a person totally unable to make a decision. I clung to the hope that I would die of a broken heart and join my husband. No such luck!

Reality should have set in sooner than it did. I lived in la-la land. Everything in our home remained the same. I even kept his cell phone charging on the counter. I came out of retirement and returned to work four weeks post shiva. When I was at work, things seemed unchanged. I worked long hours and dreaded going home to an empty house. I said Mourner's Kaddish daily for one year and visited his grave every week.

For some reason, I still find some comfort standing at his gravesite, sharing life with him.

You never know how

strong you are until being strong

is the only choice you have

-- Bob Marley

I finally admitted to myself that I was a widow and looked into and joined a widow group at the synagogue. It was one of the best decisions I could have ever made. The women in the group saved my sanity and my life. How wonderful to be surrounded by women who understood how I felt without explanation. How wonderful not to feel like a third wheel in life. How great to find a group of compassionate, strong, understanding women who became my friends. These women gave me the strength to grieve, to take one day at a time, to undergo major surgery alone, to continue living, and to finally retire and face my life. This group is what it is because of the woman at the helm. She is a retired school teacher who became a widow at a younger age. There are no words that can truly describe who she is and what she means to all of us.

I have been a widow for 5.5 years now. There is no book of rules that tells us when/how to do what. We all grieve at our own pace. While I finally moved his slippers from the bedside to the closet, I have not had the strength or desire to remove his clothes from the house. In the last few months, I finally gave myself permission to lay/sleep on his side of the bed. I talk to him constantly to share the good and negative happenings within the family. I'm still waiting for a response! I celebrate his birthday every year along with our anniversary.

Recently, I have indulged myself in a childhood fantasy to play a musical instrument. I have been taking cello lessons for the past six months. At 73 years old, I think I am the oldest beginner cellist. Hopefully, with time and much practice, I will show some accomplishment. Playing/practicing the cello brings me peace. I have also talked about owning a dog to have company in the house. Hopefully, I am smart enough not to act on that desire.

I have been told we get three choices in life; give up, give in, or give it all you've got. I am struggling to give it all I have got, working hard to hold my ground and continue to move forward. I know that does not mean I won't slip backward, all I can do is try to stay focused and go on with life knowing Bernie will be in my heart forever.

People will come and go in your life

but the person you see in the mirror

will be there forever...

Be kind to the person in the mirror!

-- Zig Ziglar

MY JOURNEY: SO-O-O GET ON WITH YOUR LIFE!

$\backsim\!\!\!\!\!\!\sim$

SANDRA BUSH KUBY

PRELUDE:

*G*rief is a solitary thing. Individuals, who undergo similar experiences, will process the events through their own personal realities. Because they grapple with mutual struggles, one widow's journey can impact others. Those who explore different paths toward healing can discover new, illuminating vistas. Increased comprehension will increase coping skills! A universal experience that widows share is a sense of isolation. After the enfolding togetherness by the rituals of death, a cloud of aloneness descends, desolation envelopes. By sharing common concerns and issues, widows can forge a way forward past society's impediments.

I was a depression era baby—endowed with an unusual upbringing by young parents, rebellious of their Euro-Jewish tribal customs. They coined their child-rearing philosophy, "interested neglect". I had no 'thou shalts', no imposed goals, few restrictions! Before the word prevailed in the vernacular, I was envied by peers for having 'cool' parents. Contradictorily, my father–a quintessential Scott Fitzgerald character–called himself "a three-time-loser" to commiserate the fact that he had three daughters. A self-made businessman, his maxims were: "Don't be a leaner!" and "Go for new experiences!" True to his convictions, he surprised us teens with a thrilling airplane trip. Where? From Philly to NYC–just for the weekend! He squired us to a Boadway show, then to Billy Rose's Diamond Horseshoe nightclub, where he ordered a Manhattan cocktail for me, saying, "You'll be going out with college boys soon, so you better learn how to drink"!

I grew up in the post-World War II years, an era pervaded by a national yearning for peace, prosperity, and normalcy. At a Sunday sorority tea dance, a dental student's opening gambit was, "Did anyone ever tell you that you have a beautiful bite?" He then confided, "All I want is a house in the suburbs, two cars in the driveway, a membership in a country club, and ten thousand a year". Conversely, expectations for college-educated females were clearly diminished. To us seniors, the male dean of the University of Pennsylvania's College for Women, offered no consideration of what might be our aspirations for the future. Neither academic nor career counseling was proposed. Nor were avenues for admission to graduate schools presented to us. Implicit was the prevalent conception that a young woman's work-life would expire with her marriage. Despite attainment of a university degree, her primary role was perceived to be that of a helpmate to an ambitious, achieving husband. In fact, many men of the time felt threatened that a working wife would diminish their prosperity index.

Preempting a segue from parents to husband, I decided to head for a writing career in New York. Major Manhattan magazines and advertising agencies merely offered girls receptionist jobs, which propelled me into the fashion world. Naively, under the guise of self-sufficiency, I turned down a job at Harper's Bazaar, because it paid five dollars less per week than the no-name agency I ultimately accepted. Eventually, lured home by my about-to-be-drafted boyfriend, Ben, I married at age twenty-two—barely before one can develop a personal identity! With enthusiastic complicity, my role evolved into that of wife to a dynamic lawyer, mother to four engaging children, manager of a city house, a beach house, and a ski house. Vision fulfilled–?!?

Although I relished my pampered lifestyle, it proved to be not enough! I channeled my creative energies into volunteer community work: public relations and production of programs for non-profit institutions. Primarily, I participated as an officer on various boards of trustees, including the National Women's Political Caucus and American ORT

(Organization for Rehabilitation through Training). Further, I served as the president of the University of Pennsylvania College Alumni Society and of the Allens Lane Art Center, where I designed "Kaleidoscope", an after-school creative program for children of working parents. As a founding vice president of the National Museum of American Jewish History, I originated its "Contemporary Artifacts" craft show and "A Place To Be On December 25th", featuring fun family projects. These events attracted thousands of participants. "You were never home!" one daughter remonstrated. When offered a paying job with an interfaith organization, my loving, fifties-era husband dismissed it with the retort, "You'll put me in a higher tax bracket!"

We lived in a couples world. While each had personal friends and activities, our social life revolved around mingling with other couples. We became part of a monthly Discussion Group, which entailed the presentation of an interesting speaker or program. This format counteracted previous two-pronged gatherings–where husbands conversed on one side of the room, while on the other, wives compared toilet training. Life proceeded in the oft-touted integrated neighborhood of West Mt. Airy, an integral part of Philadelphia's political powerhouse area–laced with U.S. senators, mayors, judges and sundry district attorneys. Having met as camp counselors, we savored summers at Rocky Dale, an enclave of twenty six rustic cabins surrounding a lake–a rudimentary, create-it-yourself camp. Typically, our kids repurposed defunct 'shanty-town' area cabins into club houses, furnished with flea market cast-offs. A converted barn, which sported a funky kitchen and a stage, served as an all-purpose social hall for performers' musicals, folk-dancing, and original satiric productions. Decades later, Rocky Dale embodies a still-in-touch extended family that spans generations. Of the original couples, only four widows remain.

Suddenly, on the cusp of early retirement, my invincible husband developed incurable cancer. Ben had been a golden boy at competitive Central High—an academic achiever, class president, athlete, editor-in-chief, and voted 'most popular' by his peers. He was the first Temple University graduate to win the coveted University of Pennsylvania Law School Faculty Scholarship. The unspoken mantra of his immigrant parents could have been: "The Cossacks are coming! The Nazis are coming!" Their son evolved into a fiercely protective force—great for his family, great for the law! Ben's parents lived their lives defensively, a background that totally contravened mine. I never owned a key, since our door was never locked. Whereas, one blizzardy night, when I dropped off my brawny boyfriend, I spied a figure scurry up the stairs. Heading home, I called my parents from a phone booth to reassure them, which consequently, produced the admonition, "Don't ever again wake us up at one a.m."! In time, Ben's parents died naturally of old age, while my type-A-personality father burned out at age fifty-three. Subsequently, I quipped, "You have the good genes—but the second wife isn't getting my jewelry"! His lawyerly retort:

"You can't rule from the grave!" Oh, how I miss that affectionate banter.

Newly bereaved, I vowed to maintain normalcy. During one of the obligatory dining out invitations, I endured a mortifying discussion by a trio of husbands, who debated how to split four credit cards seven ways. I learned to bring cash. Occasionally, compelled to call a male acquaintance for technical advice, it was interpreted as a ploy. Necessity demanded that I redefine myself as a singular, independent entity. Inevitably, I left some fabric of my life ravel away. With it went some people. It was time to reweave a new future. It was time to create a new normal.

EPILOGUE:

As widows steer through the desolation of grief, they are challenged to rechart wavering social and emotional pathways. The process of restructuring, after the loss of a lifetime partner, is different for women than for men. Immediately, widowers are umbrellaed by do-gooders and fixer-uppers. They are deluged by eager volunteers, vying for an available mate. Conversely widows, who emerge from padded cocoons, can find themselves cut adrift. Predating the feminist era of the nineteen sixties and seventies, few women built affinity groups of professional colleagues, accessible for support. A universal truism: friendship develops and solidifies between people, who share common interests. Collaborators, who dig in with commitment, will reap revitalized energy and fresh resources. In every new activity participants can plant roots that germinate new friendships. Widows, who cultivate fulfilling endeavors, will harvest blossoming opportunities for inspiration and growth. To help others, ultimately helps oneself. Just try it!

ABOUT THE AUTHOR

Sandra Bush Kuby
B.A. University of Pennsylvania
Post Graduate Certificate of Design Moore College of Art

My heart is missing
I keep hoping I'll find it
It belongs with me

It's a couple world
I used to be a member
I've been evicted

A happy moment
Just enjoy it while it lasts
It might bring you peace

Climb out of your hole
Ready to reach a mountain
Let the work begin

If you've never failed
You haven't picked such grand goals
Failure helps you win

Eternally young
Survive all of the messy bits
Try to learn from them

NAVIGATING BACK TO A MEANINGFUL LIFE

❧

MARILYN MASON

BRAVING THE UNKNOWN

Darkness descending
No way for light to seep in
I can't see a path

My existence felt hollow; I didn't care much about anything and I didn't think I ever would again. One of my first realizations that I was connecting to life again was during a visit to my therapist. She called me brave. It was difficult to connect that word to my world of pain. Yet the concept remained with me; and, at times, in between the intense and unremitting sadness, I felt a tiny bit of the bravery she ascribed to me just for continuing to go on. But go on to what or where? It seemed anywhere I was eventually headed was nowhere I wanted to be.

Why was I called brave? I told my therapist I was frightened about turning off the television one night but felt I had to because it was late and I had to get up early the next day. The TV distracted me from my grief and having to relive every part of my loss over and over. As my therapist listened, I thought she was going to commiserate with me. Instead, she shockingly said that I was brave. Over time, that word had an impact on me. As I thought about it, I felt more confident and forward-thinking. Getting up and moving is difficult–some days more than others. To all of you who push through difficult days or even minutes, consider the courage it takes and give yourself permission to think of yourself as brave.

This poem by Joanna inspired me along the way:

In the early morning hour I am aware

There is more to my life than what seems unfair.

CONTINUING CAUTIOUSLY

Bursts of light peek in
Too much for me to bear now
Do return again

I stopped seeing my therapist a year and a half after my husband's passing. I knew I had progressed somewhat but genuinely thought I had reached the end of that road. However, at the end of my third year of widowhood, I realized I was more hopeful and wanted her to know how I had processed her guidance and had moved forward. I wrote to her. I told her I was in a different place but still relying on the coping mechanisms she had taught me. She would often address the opposing thoughts that entered my mind by stretching out her hands, palms facing up and alternating up and down movements while explaining how it was possible to hold two opposing thoughts in your head at the same time and feel they were both valid. I recall thinking about this at dinner with my new friends from the W Connection, also widowed, while we were laughing and having fun. As the need arose, one of us would mention a spouse's birthday or anniversary or something else of significance and sadness joined us at the table alongside the laughter. We all very much missed our spouses. As time passed, even as I continued to long for my spouse, I began to value my privacy and enjoy the peace of my home where things were as I wanted them to be. Making my own decisions became empowering.

FULL CIRCLE

Sunshine streaming in
My journey continues now
See me, I am here

I'm a volunteer now for the W Connection, a peer group of widows helping widows. It was at about the four year mark that I began to think about giving back and was propelled by a friend who wanted to volunteer too. I could easily recapture my feelings of despair, as if I was back at the beginning of my journey in those dark days filled with pain. I believed this empathy would be an asset in dealing with new widows who were experiencing such raw and painful emotions. It's difficult to witness the despair but so very rewarding when you bring even a tiny bit of hope into someone else's darkest days. As is often said by others, I feel like "I'm paying it forward."

How did I get to this newest stage in my life? Was it the support of my new circle of widowed friends? Was it my family and other life-long friends? My therapist made a difference, even if I didn't fully realize it at the time. Maybe it was the passage of time and would have happened no matter what. Even if I had known that at the time, I didn't want to and felt I couldn't go through my grief alone. I sought help immediately from every source I mentioned above. The importance of each and every outreach has never diminished. Please remember that whatever you decide, seeking help is an act of courage, an act of faith, and you are very brave for taking that step.

The women in this book who are sharing their stories were so instrumental in helping me to take the steps I needed to take. They felt like big sisters and I prayed I could follow in their footsteps, even when I felt very little, if any, hope at all. It just didn't seem possible early on. Early on means something different to each of us. A year can be early on to one widow and two or more to another. There are no rules. This is your journey. Do it your way and think of yourself as a brave traveler.

Happy to tell you
The good memories return
Never really lost

RANDOM MUSINGS AFTER A DECADE OF WIDOWHOOD

❧

TOBIE SCHUPACK

RECLAIMING MY ANNIVERSARY

*M*y wedding day was amazing, even after a highly stressful week of snow and ice daily, an airline strike, and my mother-in-law's sudden illness and hospitalization (on the wedding day). She came to the wedding and stoically walked down the aisle, posing for pictures before returning to her hotel. We later learned she had a heart attack, but no one told us until we returned from our honeymoon.

Tom and I spent 35 anniversaries together. Like most couples, we had our ups and downs over the years, much of which later on had to do with Tom's declining health and cognitive issues. But we had a great last couple of anniversaries—especially our 35th, which was a total surprise party thrown by our wonderful kids.

Our synagogue does a monthly blessing for couples celebrating their anniversaries. Ours, at the end of December, was not exactly crowded, but we looked forward to being called forward with a few other couples each year to receive a blessing and a song from our congregational family.

We got 35 years together. Not too bad. In fact, I'd say we were both a bit surprised that we made it through some of the trials to still celebrate together. But fate decided that 35 was it, and I set off on my solo journey as a widow.

After seven years, during which my kids always made sure we celebrated what was now MY anniversary, I finally had a WTF moment.

My wedding and marriage were truly a huge deal in my life. But when a spouse dies, you get excommunicated from anniversary recognition. No more blessings or anniversary cards. No more hubby. No more coupleness.

So tomorrow, my bestie and I are spending my anniversary with a movie, a great meal, good conversation, and a lot of laughs. And we agreed to do it again on her anniversary— which will be her first without her sweetie.

I am reclaiming my anniversary as the single woman I am. I have lots of memories to smile over, some to laugh out loud about (you had to know my crazy husband), and maybe a few tears to shed. But December 27 belongs to me for always. There's a guy in heaven who can celebrate however they do up there, but I'm carrying his heart with me tomorrow so he can still be along for the ride.

I may no longer be coupled, but I am still anniversarying. And it feels great.

Maybe Hallmark should create a new card—here's to someone who was once loved mightily. Happy anniversary of the day you were married, because we care that you carry on with style, grace, and your own fumbling meshugas. Kudos to you!

ON LOSING COUPLEHOOD

We were blessed to find our spouses and have the time we did with them. Now we are making our way in this world on our own and doing very well, but challenges arise that are sometimes mini stabs to the heart.

Being part of a couple is a wonderful thing. You have found your beloved. You have someone to share your life with, all its ups and downs. You have a rhythm, a style, a home, a social life. You are blessed.

You also have lots of single friends with whom you, both husband and wife, have a great relationship. Lots of fun and laughs. You love them, and they love you.

Something happened the other day that made me think about this couple thing. I was at an event with another widow friend of mine. We were greeted so warmly by friends and were in the middle of a great conversation when the wife excused herself because she wanted to see if another couple wanted to go out to dinner with them that night. In the midst of laughing and having fun with both husband and wife, the couple chose to seek out another couple.

What is it that drives a couple to have to multiply by twos when you already have your special someone that you will be going home with? What is it that prompts couples to excommunicate their single friends in the midst of having a wonderful time with them? Why is it that couples want to date other couples?

Here is another example. About five years ago, I was at a weekly event where many people go out to dinner afterwards —no problem with that. Two female friends (both married) greeted me warmly, and we were in the middle of talking when they paused to check to see if a male friend—married but whose wife was not at this event—wanted to join them for dinner. These are good friends of mine. I was stunned and seriously wondered if I had turned invisible. I was so hurt that I did not attend for the rest of that summer. I let it get to me, which I regret, and I never said anything to them, which I also regret. In this case, the man who was part of a couple, despite the absence of his spouse—someone who had someone to go home to—was included. The coupleless me was not.

I am not whining. I have wonderful friends and family who sustain me and make life a joy. I am merely observing that couples seem to need to date each other as though they are looking for someone. I know all these people adore me, but I wonder about the dynamic of couples needing to multiply by two—and the two need to be a couple.

FINE, THANK YOU, I LIED

It is so automatic. Something that comes out of our mouths without thinking. My mother-in-law, whose brilliant brain was reduced by age and illness to the point that she couldn't speak and didn't seem to know what was going on around her, would still answer that she was fine, thank you, when asked. Her doctor let us know that it was essentially an autonomic response and not a sign that she was getting better.

Women are especially likely to want to please people by giving an expected answer. Often, we simply don't want to open ourselves up to deeper conversation. So when asked how we are, we say "Fine, thank you" or at least something like "I am doing ok."

It really didn't hit me how much I did this until I was at an event and a casual friend looked me right in the eye and asked the right question: How are you doing, really? Something in her directness prompted me to say that I was muddling through as best I could, but it was a struggle.

That moment of openness has brought me tremendous rewards. It turns out that one of her closest friends started and facilitated a group for widows who were struggling to move forward in their lives. This was not a bereavement group. It was a group centered on rebuilding your life in your new reality. When she told me this, I jumped at the opportunity to join.

This amazing group of women, headed by the woman who organized this very book, has refreshed my spirit and helped me find my voice as a strong woman who happens to be a widow. The unexpected joy is how much laughter there is among this group of women who never wanted to be widows. We grow and learn, laugh and sometimes cry, take new risks (like sharing our souls in this book), and support each other. We each have our moments of strength and times when we need to lean on each other.

So, where am I on this "Fine, thank you" thing today? After my older brother died, my sister-in-law came up with a response that truly resonates with me. She would answer, "I'm fine—every other day." There is so much honesty in that reply. It says I'm ok, but I'm not always ok. It tells people not to worry about you but that you do need their support.

I think what I am saying ties right into the title of this book. The truth is that over time, we learn to struggle pretty well, although with less and less effort over time. We grow, we hang onto our best memories, we live on to teach our grandchildren about their funny grandpa, and we find new joys in our lives. We still struggle but are doing darn well most of the time. We learn how to ask for what we need, even if it is just by subtly letting people know that we are fine— every other day.

AM I ANGRY THAT HE LEFT ME?

Each of us is unique. We have our own ways of looking at ourselves, our lives, and our situations. I know of some widows who are angry at their husband for leaving them, as though he consciously packed his bags and moved out. They are angry that their spouse died and are having trouble forgiving him for leaving them alone.

Right after Tom died, a friend also lost her husband, who had been healthy until a terrible allergic reaction took his life. We began this unwanted journey through grief together. As we moved in similar volunteer and life circles, it was quite natural that we should begin to spend a lot of time together. After a time, a clergy friend posed this question: Why is it, he asked, that so many widows step away from activities and seem to disappear for at least a while? He had noticed that we carried on and remained active, and he wondered what made the difference.

My friend and I began to think about it and realized that we shared a similar philosophy. In my mind, Tom wasn't entirely gone. When I heard a funny joke or a bit of fun gossip, I would mentally think, I bet you enjoyed that one, didn't you, honey? I felt that Tom was cheering me on, shaking his head when I made a faux pas and providing comfort when I needed an extra boost. No, I never thought he was really there. I just continued to picture us on the same team. And then, I learned that my friend felt exactly the same way about her spouse.

Even though I had plenty of times in my grief that I was indeed mad at him, sometimes for really good reason, I never was mad at him for leaving because I felt him there in my heart. I saw his eyes in the grandson that came along a couple of years later, who talks about Grandpa Tom as if he knows him—because we talk about Tom and the funny, silly, kind, caring, goofy things he said and did.

I have no real wisdom to offer as we each need to find our way on this journey we didn't want. But I hope that other widows can learn to hold their love in their hearts, to laugh at good memories, to share juicy gossip, and to hang on to that love—work at letting anger go and make room for your new self. You were part of a great team for a long time. Set anger free to drift away and cling like heck to life. I still see Tom in my grandson's eyes – and that is everything.

ABOUT THE AUTHOR

Tobie Schupack is a marketing research consultant who has missed her husband of 35 years for just over a decade. Tom began his struggle with bipolar depression when their children were young and later had lasting physical and organ issues related to brain injury. Despite their ups and really down downs, Tobie and Tom had an amazing time together. Since his passing, Tobie has focused on family, a greater role in volunteering, finding her voice, and realizing her own strength as an independent woman. As someone who used to worry about whether people would like her, Tobie has made it her goal to speak up for herself and for others. She continues to work on trying to be the wonderful woman her husband thought she was.

You can't save someone
They must do it for themselves
Be there for support

I hear new music
I am open to the sound
My life is changing

Go back to before
Is not a possible move
Must live in the now

I'm single again
After a lifetime of love
I don't know the rules

I've just been thinking
Did I always wear a mask
Or is it just now

I'm my own person
Trying to find my own way
Through the confusion

TEARS AND JOY

A DIFFERENT KIND OF "HAPPY"

BARBARA TALLERMAN

*G*rief is an experience that we each feel at one time or another during our personal journey through life. Generally, It's about loss—the loss of a family member, a spouse, or a pet. It can be about the loss of freedom during the Covid pandemic and the dreaded isolation from family and friends, money, a job, or a possession—even a reputation or pride.

But grief can also tie us together:

To the women who have shared their personal stories on these pages about how they "creatively" processed their own stages of grief, I say, "Thank you. I will always be grateful for your support, your encouragement, and your commitment to making sure that as vulnerable as I felt, I knew that I was not alone and that there really was a path forward to a sense of peace."

I am an elderly woman who, through the ages, did experience all the losses I mentioned above. When my beloved father started acting strangely in the late 70s, at age 78, I would call him during the day while my mother was at work to ask how he was doing. I remember how his response was so mystifying, "I'm fine, dear. I'm here with my friends." I did hear voices in the background, and finally realized that his "friends" were on the TV. It wasn't until the night that he got out of bed to pee in the corner of the living room on the brand new carpet that I realized we needed help. The doctor simply said, "What do you expect? He's old."

It wasn't that Dad died in March of 1980 that led to loss and grief, it was the fact that we lost him years before when he pulled a napkin out of his pocket and handed me "a million dollars."

In September of that year, I read an article in *The New York Times* with a headline, "Dementia is not a sign of aging. It is a disease called 'Alzheimer's.'" I was enraged. I knew there was more to this behavior other than his age, so I joined a class called "Writing Our Personal Story." It took me a year and a half to write a 299-page book about how Alzheimer's can destroy a family. I even had an agent to take it on. By then, though, the market had become oversaturated with these findings. The good news is that processing my sadness through this journal allowed me to come to terms with my anger and grief over the lack of medical help at the time and my fury toward my mother for constantly calling Dad "crazy."

Unlike other painful losses, when my husband passed in 2012, I was traumatized by the reality that I was then a "me," after 32 years of being a "we." I doubted my ability to function without Marvin at my side. During that most difficult and confusing time, I continually asked myself, "Who am 'I'?"

That led to another question: "Who **was** I?" What were the things I embraced as I grew? Besides writing, I became passionate about photography in the early 80s, computers in 1985, and, in 1996, the Internet when it was initially introduced as a viable option for commerce and community involvement. With courage and creativity, what began as hobbies became two small startup businesses that I nurtured for twenty-plus years.

While rummaging through my past, I regained the confidence to go forward as a "me."

Thinking creatively can show up at the most unexpected times and in a myriad of ways.

Looking back to the things that have always brought you joy is the greatest start to overcoming the pain you may feel now. If you like to paint, paint; if you were an avid reader, read; sing out loud if singing is what you love to do. You have talents!

Explore them and be amazed at how these expressions can soften any blow.

Until I met the women who participated in this book, I had never heard the word, "haiku," an ancient form of Japanese poetry that expresses an entire thought in a total of 17 syllables in just 3 lines of text, the first line containing 5, the second 7, and the third 5.

Here's an example of a haiku explaining how to write a haiku:

Write in syllables

Five-Seven-Five says it all

As clear as need be

Haiku can be about grief, loss, or anything that you see or feel. It is a creative way to simplify your imagination and your observance of life itself. I urge you to try it—you may be happily surprised at how simplicity can uplift your spirit.

During the pandemic:
I do my best when
Living through this Covid threat
Grateful for today

Beginning of Spring:
Squirrels hide their food
Flowers bloom while sweet birds sing
Hope is in the air

On a trip to Machu Picchu, Peru:
Woman with child
Shows gratitude for our help
As she begs for food

As step-mother to my husband's 3 children, I was fortunate to be part of a growing family that now includes 7 grandchildren and 7 great grandchildren. Marvin is deeply missed by all. It was only after coming across a cartoon of "Winnie the Pooh" which read "I didn't realize we were making memories, I just thought we were having fun," that I was prompted to gather together dozens of photos taken over the years which were filled with family fun and turned them into memories in a multi-page paper scrapbook. Although this project took 6 months from start to finish, it made me smile. Each "grand" family received a copy, which was acknowledged with both **tears and joy**.

For Marvin:
Loved you to the sky
Now you're up there forever
Living in my heart

For me:
I am not broken.
But sometimes I think I am.
All I need is glue

"Glue" comes in many forms. For me, it was keeping busy. The distraction and diversion of creating some things new has allowed me to transform my sorrow into a **"different kind of 'happy.'"**

For you:
Shed your tears with love
Live a little every day
Joy will come your way

THIS MOMENT MATTERS

JANE KRAMER

This moment matters
Dream of the growth you want to live
You have the power

*L*ife with my husband Jeff was an amazing roller coaster. He was a gifted man and instantly beloved by many who met him. Four years since Jeff's passing, I still encounter people who met him once and have never forgotten his ability to engage with them. Jeff was complex. I loved him even when my heart ached because of many life events that were challenging and scary. In 2016, the most difficult challenge of our lives began—a diagnosis of ALS. Jeff lost nearly all of his bodily functioning over the next twenty-seven months. We enjoyed our time together as much as we could. We traveled with the family, reminisced, and recounted many of the special moments of our years together—nearly 40. As the disease progressed, we experienced all the layers of the complexity of our relationship. After Jeff's passing, that left me working through the waves of grief, sadness, fear, and longing for my lost love. I needed a way to move forward.

Through Life Coach training in 2009, I learned that for me, the answer to navigating the bumps in the road is to strive to live in the moment by releasing judgment and realizing that the only thing I can really control in life is my thoughts. Since then, I have been thirsty for knowledge about how the mind works and how to release the worry that held me back. As a tween, I learned basic yoga at school. Little did I know then how precious that experience was. Yoga became my balancing practice for most of my adult years. After Jeff passed, I fulfilled my dream of pursuing yoga teacher training. I am so appreciative that I was able to have an in-person experience right before the pandemic. Throughout the pandemic, the mat has been my magic carpet to some peace and release, both physically and emotionally. My yoga practice and talk therapy have helped me to frame my life with Jeff as a trove of loving memories that I can feel grateful for. Gratefulness has become my spiritual uplift no matter what setbacks I encounter, and I have had some recently! I think of Jeff and appreciate my ability to walk, talk, eat and smile. That helps me put life into perspective pretty quickly.

I consider my children and grandchildren to be "the jewels in my crown". My heart bursts with love, admiration, and gratitude when I think of them. Often I pinch myself because of the gift of having them in my life. I think about how proud Jeff would be, and it gives me an inner smile. I also love to reach out to my extended family and connect with them as often as I can. My family has enhanced my life and adds to the cornucopia of gratitude I try to consciously access. My children help keep me balanced. I confer with them on many decisions in my life.

While I still have dear friends who are married, I have developed many new connections with widows who have enhanced my life and helped to support me in my journey to rebuild my life. Our shared experience gives me a feeling of being understood even when we are not talking about our common loss. The women writers of this book are thoughtful and charged with the

desire to move forward with purpose. In this chapter of my life, I am taking the time to stay present and search for my life purpose that is most meaningful right now. I often need to pause and give myself permission to take care of myself in order to heal and grow. I am excited about

the potential of my life even though I have not yet firmed up my path—I acknowledge that the ideas keep evolving and that I should give them room to morph into what they are meant to be.

Sometimes I react to things too quickly without my partner to bounce my thoughts off of. I am trying to be aware when that happens and slow myself down. Admittedly, that skill is a work in progress. I try to remind myself to cut myself slack. As you can see, I have oodles of self-talk. I also talk to my doggy, Millie. I always say how happy I am to have had her by my side for eight years now. She is my precious companion.

I spent my adult life as a "we". Now I am trying to learn more about myself and my "who" as an independent woman. I feel so fortunate to have this opportunity. One might call this a silver lining. I feel that it is all in how I perceive life. I am acutely aware of the power I have to build my world and that it will take my engagement and intention. I am excited about life and all of its possibilities. Now it is time to meditate on that thought. This moment matters.

Death does not end life
It brings out the best in us
To cherish the past

I hate to complain
But I am over my head
I think I am drowning

My world has become
A million broken pieces
Please give me some glue

Have a new vision
The mist will clear very soon
Open and aware

I am heartbroken
But I won't become bitter
I promised myself

Something has happened
It's a life changing event
I hope I survive

THROUGH A SEVEN YEAR LENS

❧

DID BECOMING A WIDOW CHANGE ME?

*a*t one time, this question seemed reasonable. It seemed like something to consider. It seemed like I would find a meaningful answer to the question if I gave it enough thought. It also seemed like the definitive answer would certainly be "yes." How could it not be "yes?"

However, upon reflection, there then arose a new question: "What doesn't change us?"

Change is inevitable. Everything is changing all the time; it is our moment-by-moment reality. We would be changed even if our beloved spouses were still present because all of life is a process of flux and change.

Yes, my marital status has changed. Yes, my day-to-day activities have changed. My skin, eyesight, hair, and muscle tone have all changed. The Covid pandemic has wrought an unexpected myriad of changes for all of humanity. There's no way to circumvent, halt, or influence any of it (not even with Botox!). One cannot hide from it nor wish it away.

Accepting impermanence and not holding tightly to yesterday has been a blessing for me. I am in the process of realizing that all that I have right now is appreciated with immense gratitude, but any piece of it may break, wear out, or disappear tomorrow. To let go of the past does not suggest forgetting it, but it does suggest the need to recognize our tendency to yearn for the old. When we grasp at the desire to rewrite history, hoping to roll back the clock and alter the outcome, we create our own suffering. I have found it helpful (in this learning process) to notice this desire without judgment—just see it for what it is. It's not right or wrong. It's just a thought that arises and will pass if I don't dwell on it.

I've listened to friends talk of things that "shouldn't have happened". Others speak often of their loss and ongoing pain. I too have done these things. I hope we all may someday be free of this pain and suffering and that each of us will abandon our "shoulds" and "should nots". The cause of our pain, sadness, anger, fear, anxiety is not solely tied to the loss of a spouse. Yes, that loss is truly and deeply sad-even heart-wrenching- and it requires a period of grieving and often painful adjustment. There will be good days and not so good days. That's how life works for all of us. However, continuous suffering comes from letting our emotions and cravings take charge and push us around in a whirlwind. Since yesterday's events were always out of our control, nor can they be changed, we can loosen their grip on us.

Again, **letting go doesn't mean "forget your husband".**

None of this is easy. It's a difficult uphill climb with frequent backsliding, but if we notice that we let go for a moment, that's an accomplishment. We can meet this moment with peace and kindness.

Let's all find love and compassion for ourselves and see the light of day. We each will continue to remember our husbands with gratitude for their presence in our lives and cherish our memories. Let's do so without the suffering of clinging to an alternate reality. Let's be patient with ourselves and take baby steps towards the freedom from wanting.

There may be a heart-mind space still occupied by a spouse, but there are also many other spaces to fill with love and joy.

<u>Love After Love</u> by Derek Walcott
The time will come
When, with elation
You will greet yourself arriving
At your own door, in your own mirror
And each will smile at the other's welcome,

And say, sit here. Eat.
You will love again the stranger who was yourself.
Give wine. Give bread. Give back your heart
To itself, to the stranger who has loved you

All your life, whom you ignored
For another, who knows you by heart.
Take down the love letters from the bookshelf,

The photographs, the desperate notes,
Peel your own image from the mirror.
Sit. Feast on your life.

THROUGH A SEVEN YEAR LENS IN HAIKU

1. Winter's Journey Begins with a Crash
Today my heart broke.
Loss, despair, sadness descend.
Snowed under by grief.

Hours, days, weeks, months.
Sleepless nights keep me churning.
Grief's grip remains strong.

2. No Permanent Injuries
Hello, rays of light.
Corners of lips lifting up.
Welcome back, smiles.

Life, like flowers, blooms.
Spring is warmly seeping through.
Goodbye, dark winter.

3. A New Road Appears

Sweet sunshine greets me.
Living in its dear embrace...
Joyous, calm, at peace.
The past—now quiet.
The future—unknowable.
Now is all we have.

TEN THINGS MY HUSBAND USED TO DO (NOW I DO THEM)

• Pick-up the mail

• Clean the garage

• Prune big bushes

• Call the plumber, electrician, etc.

• Buy cell phones and computers

• Stand on a 6-foot ladder to change light bulbs

• Remember everyone's birthday

• Buy wine

- Drive at night

- HUG ME!

UNDOING A LIFE AND THINGS I DIDN'T KNOW

HILLARY OSER

One of the most difficult things to do after a death is undoing a life. Whether it is done right away or down the road, you find the strength to do it.

Which is worse, a long lingering death or a sudden death? Both suck for certain, but sudden is worse when you need to undo life. There are no last notes, no important info provided, no "what abouts"; just a life to undo—business, personal, financials.

My husband died suddenly—a heart attack at 62. The day started as a beautiful Sunday morning. We were at our synagogue doing a mitzvah (good deed), cleaning the kitchens with other members. By Sunday afternoon, he was gone. Telling my girls (ages 20 and 22) and the family was grueling, but it had to be told. We'll get through this together, I said, with some help from family and friends.

The burial is over, the shiva is over, the people stop calling, and now what?...

HIS LIFE—WHERE TO START UNDOING IT.

Luckily, I could rely on his co-workers to undo his real estate business. He had clients to tell and to reassign, things I couldn't do. But they had questions, what do I think about—where is—I don't really know or care, my husband just died. You put on the face and try to be polite and give answers or try to help. Eventually, business affairs get completed, and that's the last you hear from anyone in that world.

Financially I always paid the household bills, so that was no problem, but there were business bills to deal with. There was a life insurance policy, website bills, and credit card bills to pay. Who knew credit card companies would negate the bill after a death? I paid it, but what were these recurring charges? Detective work and a lot of phone calls gave me the answers, and people were nice enough to tell me how to end the charges. He was paying to keep his top position on a website that I knew nothing about. I now know these placements are expensive and can be sold. And don't ask me about computer sites and passwords—it's a bit of a nightmare. My girls and I had a "fun" time trying to guess passwords to get anyone to speak with us to cancel accounts. After his death, I couldn't be more emphatic in telling people to write down passwords to make life easier later.

AND THEN THE PERSONAL STUFF

Everyone gathered around the table, children, and siblings, going through clothes, personal items—who wants what, what gets donated, what is this? What do I really want to keep? Nothing—I want my husband back. Over time it all gets done, and then the closets and drawers are empty. It took me almost a year to get the courage to put my things on his side.

The things I never knew he did or things he had until after his death. How I wish I had an hour more to ask him, "what the F". A whole drawer of family photos which I had been asking for over our 25-year marriage—he said he didn't have any. He had money (cash) he had stashed in a zippered pouch in his home office drawer. It was a nice surprise, but we probably could have used that money sooner. The certificate from the synagogue stating he did classes to make his Bar Mitzvah—I had to ask the Rabbi what this was all about. David never had a bar mitzvah, and he wanted to be more Jewish. Who doesn't have secrets—but why not tell me. I'll never know. He was who he was, and I loved him.

SO UNDOING A LIFE SUCKS

But it has to get done, and the surviving spouse generally takes the lead. There's no way around it, just go through it.

Do it on your own timetable but don't wait too long as your new altered life needs to start. I think undoing a life, while very sad, also brings fond memories and smiles, which is good for everyone. Do you remember when?

As I write this, it's been almost ten years, and I remember every detail and probably always will. I'm crying too, which I do periodically, even these many years later. What's the saying—that which doesn't kill you makes you stronger. Well, I guess I'm stronger. I'm still here, thriving, enjoying my new life. What's the alternative?

While his life is physically undone, it will never be undone mentally. He lives on in his girls and the five grandchildren that he never met.

It's complicated
Do I live my brand new truth
Or do I stay stuck

This is what I know
I've had time to be with me
I know I am better

So I will move on
Confident and much stronger
Use this time wisely

My friends are my strength
I am at peace with myself
All is well within

Honor who you were
With all of your faults and mistakes
Enjoy the new you

When life gets you down
Do not let your heart get hard
Keep it soft with love

WIDOW

❧

SHELLEY

A word that I never thought about until I became one.

Then I hated it.

I would leave forms empty where they asked for marital status.

I married young and always had someone to "take care of me."

Then I didn't.

I was scared and alone even when I was with family and friends.

All those decisions discussed between husband and wife were no longer a discussion.

It was up to me alone.

I made mistakes but continued to carry on. Each day was one foot in front of the other.

Slowly I came to realize that I could do this.

I can carry on by myself.

I am now stronger emotionally and mentally. I am more confident and surer of myself.

Even when some decisions turn out to be wrong, it often doesn't matter in the long run.

I have met a group of equally strong, intelligent women. We are a group that no woman wants to join.

We are widows. We laugh and move forward.

I now travel with a wonderful friend (hopefully will be able to travel again after covid).

Life is good once more.

Yes, I still talk to my husband and tell him that I miss him.

Life goes on.

Stay well.

WIDOW WISDOM

❧

NANA GOLDBERG

*I*F. My husband would say it was a little word with a big meaning. If only I knew then what I know now, perhaps I would harbor fewer regrets for how I acted or more so about what I did or didn't say during my marriage. But life and learning follow their path. Some of my thoughts relate very specifically to becoming a widow. Although the pain that I felt when I first checked the box for widow may also be felt by someone who now checks a box for divorced, single, retired, or unemployed. Perhaps there are some things that only relate to being widowed. But the more I think about this, I begin to think that not only widows are lonely, not only widows have to figure out how to manage everything by themselves, how to create a new identity, or what to do when their kid doesn't listen.

Some of the things I have lived through were so painful I thought I could write a book about my experience. I have come to understand, as I have worked through some of my pain, that it actually is possible in just one sentence to say, for example: My husband was born with a rare congenital heart condition—that I didn't realize how it would impact me, our son, shape the rest of his life, my life, our lives, and only give us fifteen years of marriage. I would not have thought that I could put that in one sentence, and yet there it is.

How do you transition from being a couple to being alone overnight? I didn't think about researching how to be a widow. I was too busy avoiding the fact that my chronically ill husband might die this time. In our harmonious interfaith family, he was Catholic, and my son and I are Jewish. I was immediately thrown into undertaking end of life rituals with his grieving mother and several opinionated siblings taking control of the viewing and mass. I felt like a deer caught in the headlights. They chose a ridiculous number of wreaths which, of course, I paid for. I was able to summon my strength and override their choice of a Cadillac casket. I selected a beautiful wooden style that was appropriate for a Jewish burial.

For whatever reason, he wasn't buried for seven agonizingly long days instead of almost immediately, which is the Jewish custom. I was alone most of the time, and my son and I began being a twosome at night. My mom told me he had asked years before if it was possible to be buried with our family in the Jewish cemetery. He also told me what funeral home he wanted as well as which suit he wanted to wear. He did all of this before we got the devastating news that there was nothing more the doctors could do. He was more prepared, and for that, I was grateful.

To most of those who came to pay their respects, my husband's death was a shock. I naturally take care of others before myself and found that I was comforting people who had just discovered they had lost a friend or relative. My mother-in-law kept tugging at my jacket to sit down, which was the custom, but it wasn't my nature. I longed for the human touch and was grateful for hugs, especially since we weren't surrounded by friends at a Jewish Shiva. I had already prepared my son to nod his head when he was told he would now be the head of the household. I had reassured him that it was an old saying and far from the truth.

Loss can be so overwhelming that you may lose your sense of self. I know because I became another person on the day of my husband's funeral. In order to get through this necessary and unfamiliar ordeal, I assumed the persona of the most well-known Catholic widow I could think of. I embodied the stoic grace of Jackie Kennedy, holding on to her young children's hands as I held onto my sons. I needed to emotionally remove myself to get through this ritual. I don't remember hearing the priest's words, the music, except for

Ave Maria, or the eulogies. He had wanted me to speak, but I knew that would be impossible. I easily spoke to small and large audiences—that wasn't the issue. I couldn't fathom the thought of condensing his life into ten minutes. To me, he was larger than life.

I developed widow brain. I couldn't think straight. I felt disconnected and on autopilot. Concentrating on anything for more than ten minutes was impossible. Gratefully, the lovely sympathy cards were brief. Maybe this helps protect you from your reality, like being put into an induced coma in order for the brain to recuperate. Had it not been for my young son and my family business, I doubt I would have left my now half-empty bed. That is until people remind you of your reality and life beckons.

One of the hardest parts about becoming a widow is listening to people who really don't know what to say, especially if you are young or the death is sudden and unexpected. Many of those who have not experienced the loss of a loved one yet possibly don't know what to say. If they haven't lost their partner, it may be particularly hard to find comforting words. Here are a few of the worst things I've heard in no particular order:

"You look great!" I imagine the "A" for adultery had been replaced by a "W." "You look great!" After several months I had gained twenty pounds. I still looked great!

"They're in a better place." Better than being here with our family? Better than the ups and downs of life and marriage? Better than doctor's appointments, countless tests, procedures, and operations, so they fight to live because that's what they want? How do they know it's better? Have they been there? Are they reporting back?

"I can imagine how you feel." NO, you can't! A divorce, a death of a parent, sibling, or beloved pet is not similar to the loss of what you hoped would be your lifelong partner. You're not going to be in your 80s holding hands on a park bench. Even other widows don't know exactly how you feel. But you do share an unspoken bond. We've joined the club that nobody wants to be a member of.

Eventually, people will expect your grieving to be over like it's a cold. "Aren't you done grieving yet?" They don't want to hear any more about your sadness, loneliness, fear, or see your tears. They want you to be the person you used to be before there became a huge hole in your heart. They have taken you to dinner. Duties done. Do they think I wouldn't pay for my meal in order to enjoy an evening out again? You're fortunate if your girlfriends even want to have lunch with you anymore. Some of them worry that you'll go after their husband. NO!!! You want yours to come back. And by the way, being a widow is not contagious.

We all travel a different path along our grief journey. Grief is not linear. Sometimes a good cry comes unexpectedly. If you're in public, it really makes people uncomfortable. So, what! Our loved ones may visit us in dreams. We may think we spot them in a crowd. They may come to us through pennies on the ground, seeing bright red cardinals or a blinking lightbulb. Your song comes over the speaker while you're picking up your prescription at the pharmacy. And you smile. You never thought you would smile or laugh again. But one day, you do. It doesn't mean you've stopped grieving. But maybe for a moment, you can remember what happiness feels like.

The pain of your reality often becomes clearer in the second year of widowhood. As the fog slowly lifts, you realize your partner is gone forever. They're really not coming back. You have to figure out yourself or hire someone to do the things your partner used to do. You discover things they did before that you may have taken for granted. Feelings of guilt, envy, and anger appear out of nowhere. Many women are afraid to voice these feelings out loud. Some journal, some start seeing a therapist. The fortunate ones find other widows with whom they can share their feelings.

My husband and I were fifty years old when he died. Our son was twelve. I didn't know anyone who spoke widowhood. My grieving took a backseat to raising our son and finding him an organization for children who had suffered a loss. There was a facilitator for the adults who wished to join together. It helped me understand what other children and families were experiencing. However, I couldn't relate to any of the parents or guardians. My son found solace there. As a "youngish" widow, I didn't realize I was now a single mom. It was probably because I didn't want to be one. I recently heard a widow call herself a solo mom. Solo sounds so much more appealing to me.

Three years after my loss, I joined a bereavement group for spousal support. We never saw a widower. The classes lasted six weeks. Some of us had formed a common bond, and we didn't want to lose each other. We were fortunate to have a "more experienced and stronger woman" who organized and led a monthly meeting for us to stay together.

New widows were welcomed, and our group grew. Several years later, we heard of a national organization called The W Connection. Our wonderful leader met with the directors, and we grew stronger as the first chapter outside of New York. She had been a teacher, and her creativeness and caring helped the women bond and find community. I became particularly close with her, and we always say it's so sad that we lost our husbands in order to meet and develop a very loving friendship. We have known each other for eleven years, and I don't know anyone else who understands me, comforts me, and uplifts my spirits. I hope I do the same for her.

When the pandemic began, our chapter and the national organization pivoted to Zoom meetings. I never imagined I could connect and feel warmth and compassion from the widows in the Brady Bunch squares. It's been a gift to so many who are quite alone to find a community.

My most recent loss was closing my one-hundred-year-old family retail and wholesale business. I didn't acknowledge it, but I had sunk into a different kind of coma. I had lost my career and part of my identity. It took me quite some time to realize this was a loss I needed to grieve. With help from my therapist and close friends, I applied the strategies I learned from my widowhood journey to this loss. Once again, it takes time.

The national organization invited me to train to be a volunteer facilitator for monthly Zoom topic meetings. It gave me a sense of purpose that I had lost, and I began to come out of this coma. I have met incredible women who have become my friends. Most of us have never met in person. We like to say that "We're girlfriends who get it." Volunteering helps me be there for women that weren't there in my time of need. But I have come to realize that there are many circumstances, other than becoming a widow, that beg for help and understanding. There are many new journeys as we travel through life.

Any loss has a way of magnetizing the previous ones. Your parents, a sibling, a dear friend's death, or that of a beloved pet can cause memories of your partner flooding your brain. My dear friend shared the poem "i carry your heart with me." Below is a portion of the poem that really resonated. It helped me find a place in my heart to keep my husband close. I now realize that my heart expands and makes room for me to carry more loved ones with me forever. My heart is filled with loving memories.

i carry your heart with me(i carry it in)

e.e. cummings

i carry your heart with me(i carry it in my heart) i am never without it (anywhere i go you go, my dear; and whatever is done

by only me is your doing, my darling)

here is the deepest secret nobody knows (here is the root of the root and the bud of the bud and the sky of the sky of a tree called life; which grows higher than soul can hope or mind can hide) and this is the wonder that's keeping the stars apart

i carry your heart (i carry it in my heart)

ABOUT THE AUTHOR NANA GOLDBERG

I would be remiss if I didn't acknowledge Susan Gross, the loving and courageous woman who has helped so many Philadelphia widows move forward on their journeys. She bravely agreed to lead our group and she is the glue that keeps us together. She is my dearest friend. We agree that it's so sad that we lost our husbands in order to find each other.

I welcome the opportunity to help you through this journey and join our community. Please reach out to me @ nanagoldberg1@gmail.com

They said…

They said "I am sorry for your loss"
I said " why are you sorry, did you do something wrong?"

They said " I am sorry you lost your husband"
I said " I didn't lose him...I know exactly where he is"

They said "So are you staying in your home?"
I said "sure, the minute my husband dies I am going to leave all my memories too, no I think I'll stay awhile"

They said "so are you dating again"
I said - nothing

They said " Sorry I haven't called in awhile, I didn't know what to say"
I said "How about trying...Hi How are you, Want to get coffee?"

They said " Everything happens for a reason"
I said " Tell me the reason".

They said " We all have problems"
I said " Enjoy yours".

They said " They are in a better place".
I said… no words just a breath

They said " I thought you would be over it by now".
I said " sorry to disappoint you".

They said " Now you can live your own life instead of taking care of a disabled husband".
I said… better keep my mouth shut

They said " At least you are young enough to remarry"
I said " Are you proposing".

Adnausium:: you can add your own!

YOU'RE A WIDOW

NOW WHAT?

MARY ELIZABETH

First, there are those preconceptions – your own and others':
You will never be happy again
You won't be capable of handling all of life's chores without
help
You need a partner – and help in finding one
You don't want to be around couples
And there are many more – these are just some of the more
common ones.

*N*ote: I have not distinguished between preconceptions which are yours and which are others'. There are – many - overlaps.

The most common preconception widows hear perhaps is that there is a cycle of grief which all widows experience and which is spelled out in helpful literature. Nope – no such thing. Just as we are all individuals, who share some things but not many other things, we grieve in different ways. If your partner died after a long illness, during which you were his caregiver, either sole or one of a team, your grieving experience will be different from someone whose partner died suddenly. Sudden death brings disbelief and a longer period before acceptance; it also brings more social and emotional support for a widow for some time after the death. A partner's death after a long illness can bring the survivor not only loss but a feeling of relief from a burden of caring and sympathy – and guilt about that relief. A long illness usually brings increasing isolation for the surviving caregiver and less support following the death. However, even within these two groups, grief has its own season – which does not follow the accepted timelines or shapes.

As to the rest of this type of popular wisdom, again experience varies greatly among widows, reflecting the range of individual personalities and experiences. What is common to all widows, however, is the need to reassess and redefine themselves. Part of that redefinition is task oriented; widows must assume tasks that previously were shared or handled by the other partner, often financial tasks or making major purchases. Those whose partners died after a long illness probably make that transition more gradually as their partners become more debilitated, an advantage offset by depletion from the burden of caring. This depletion often requires significant time for replenishment following the death. Sudden widows are often shocked and unable to function well, perhaps offset by the relatively greater support often available to these widows while they regain their ability to function. The common denominator is time—and the time necessary to regain the ability to accomplish necessary tasks is often much less than the time necessary for reassessment and redefinition.

What do you enjoy? Your answer previously included those activities which you enjoyed with your partner. Now you have the chance to examine that answer in a much more personal sense – what do you, yourself, enjoy? Your answer to this question will likely evolve over time. What are your strengths? Your answer to this question also will likely evolve as you develop your ability to manage necessary tasks you have not previously handled. Many widows discover new abilities and strengths as they assume these tasks, which become part of their redefinitions of themselves.

What is/are your community/ies? Sudden widows' communities have probably centered around other couples. Widows of those dying after long illness probably have diminished, perhaps nonexistent, communities. Both need to rebuild their social groups. Rebuilding communities requires time and energy and often seems daunting to the point of impossibility. However, looking for new groups offers opportunities to discover and develop your own interests and strengths. A good starting point might be a faith-based group, a hobby group, a neighborhood group or a service group working on a cause which interests you or is important to you.

Joining a group need not be a long-term commitment. Try it out to see if you find people or activities which add to your life instead of burdening it. If a group doesn't add or brings only burdens after a trial period, move on to another opportunity. As you gradually assemble your new communities, your redefinition of yourself expands. A worthy goal is a usefully busy life, not merely a busy one, but worthy goals come in many different shapes and sizes.

So, now what? Your life has changed. Sadness is real and appropriate, but you have the opportunity to reassess and redefine yourself. Take the time you need and move at your own pace as you discover and develop your next life.

Making Life Easier

- Getting the mail can be upsetting
- It is hard to make decisions alone at first
- Eating alone in the house is lonely. You might not want to sit at the table.
- If you are not a joint cardholder on your spouse's credit card you cannot use it.
- Frequent flier miles can disappear
- Speak to the spouse's employer. Make sure you know what benefits you might be entitled to.
- Find out about how to change health insurance benefits
- Check to see if you are old enough for medicare or social security
- Make sure you get enough death certificates so you can change the status on all of the charges and accounts.
- Check to see if there is a will so you know how to handle things
- Make sure you know your spouse's passwords
- Utilities, mobile phone, mortgage might need to be updated if your name is not on the bill.
- People might feel obligated to pay for you at meals so they might not ask you out
- Make sure you talk about your grief

- Don't push your feelings down. Sit down with them and talk to yourself out loud.
- Understand that some days you will feel hopeful and then the next day you might feel overwhelmed.
- Try to identify your emotions: sadness, guilt, anger, happiness
- Don't worry about what others think about how you are handling things
- Don't let any negative people in your inner circle
- Reach out and ask for help if you need it
- It is helpful to keep a journal so you can get your feelings out and keep track of your progress
- Don't judge yourself ! Just do or not do what feels right for you
- Enjoy going over happy memories in the past
- If their voice is on the answering machine it could be difficult to remove
- Holidays, rituals and happy occasions can be hard

BE SAFE AND BE WELL. WE HOPE OUR EXPERIENCES HAVE BEEN HELPFUL AND HAVE PUT YOU IN A POSITIVE AND STRONGER FRAME OF MIND. IF YOU FEEL YOU WANT TO CONNECT AND LET US KNOW HOW YOU ARE DOING WE'RE HERE! YOU ARE NOT ALONE.

SUSAN GROSS

as45@comcast.net

OUR WISH FOR YOU

Dear Readers-

We can't thank you enough for choosing to spend your time with us. We are so grateful for the chance to walk into your life at a very vulnerable time and share our experiences. We hope our loving stories will give you strength and insight as you journey through your own personal story.

OUR WISH FOR YOU

1. Let your life shine

2. Stop hiding your talents

3. Develop yourself

4. Don't live fear based

5. Focus on one thing

6. Don't worry what people think

7. A struggle or enemy force may push you to move forward

8. Stop living passively

9. Imagine where you could be next year if you took one thing and excelled at it!

Talk yourself into it!

AS ROY ROGERS SAID "HAPPY TRAILS TO YOU
UNTIL WE MEET AGAIN"
Hugs and light,

Susan J. Gross and 19 wonderful women
Check out more books to here help support you on
your journey

www.ingramcontent.com/pod-product-compliance
Lightning Source LLC
Chambersburg PA
CBHW060322050426
42449CB00011B/2615